A Year in Small Drawings

SKETCHBOOK

Editor: Karrie Witkin
Cover Design: Diane Shaw
Design: JC Lanaway
Production Manager: Denise LaCongo

ISBN: 978-1-4197-2774-0

This book was conceived, designed, and produced by
Leaping Hare Press
An imprint of The Quarto Group
The Old Brewery, 6 Blundell Street
London N7 9BH, United Kingdom
T (0)20 7700 6700 F (0)20 7700 8066
www.quartoknows.com

Printed and bound in China
10 9 8 7 6 5 4 3 2 1

ABRAMS
The Art of Books

115 West 18th Street
New York, NY 10011
abramsbooks.com

A Year in Small Drawings

SKETCHBOOK

Matilda Tristram

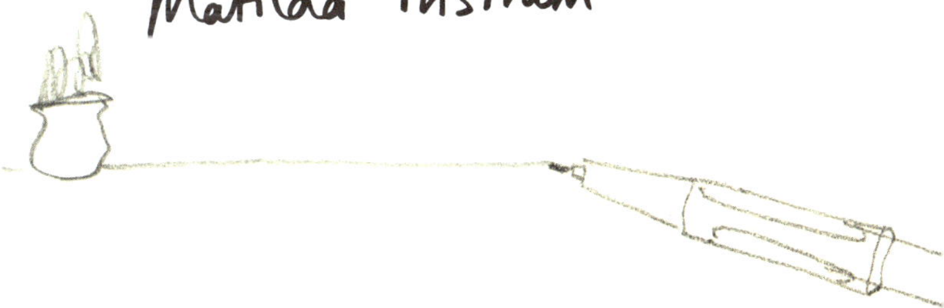

ABRAMS NOTERIE, NEW YORK

CONTENTS

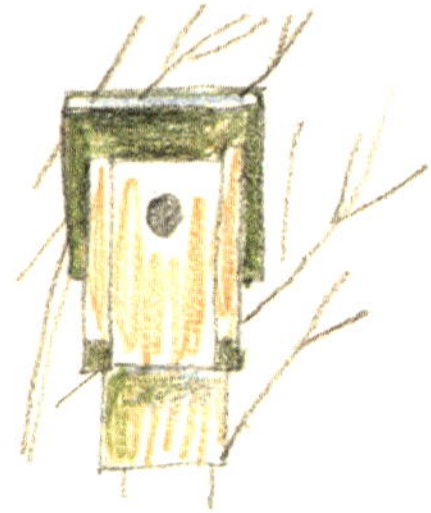

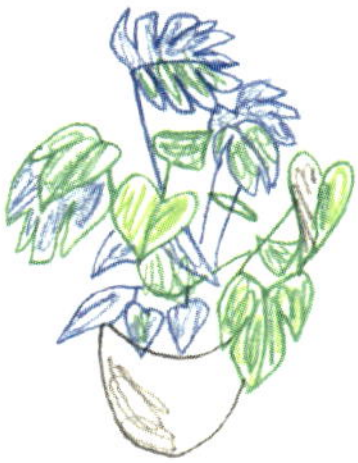

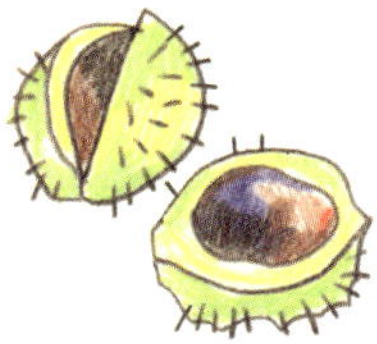

Summer

Fall

ABOUT THIS JOURNAL

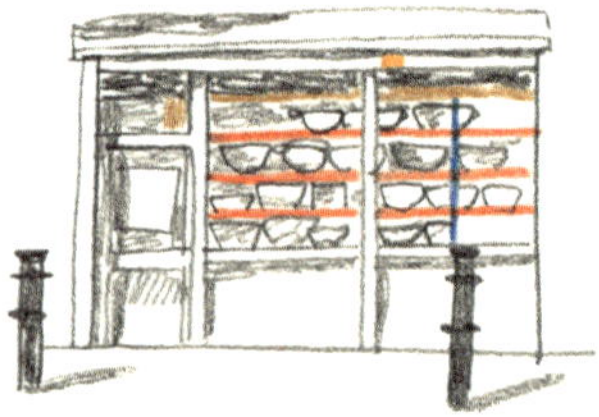

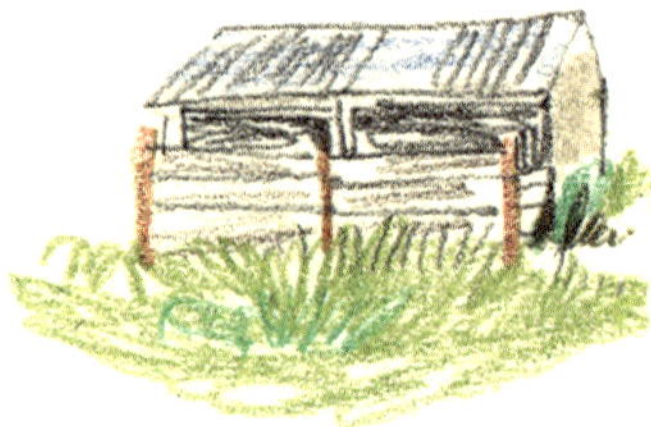

This journal is for filling with drawings of the things in your world. You can think of it as a diary and work in it every day for a year, or just use it when the mood takes you and fill it up gradually as you go along. Whichever way you choose to use it, the purpose of the journal is to encourage you to look outward, draw with purpose, and draw more often.

Look outward

A drawing can show more than simply what something looks like. It can tell stories of the places you have been to and the things you have seen. It can record moments, objects, or scenes that you want to remember. Drawing an object or place can trigger other memories that may be surprising or meaningful.

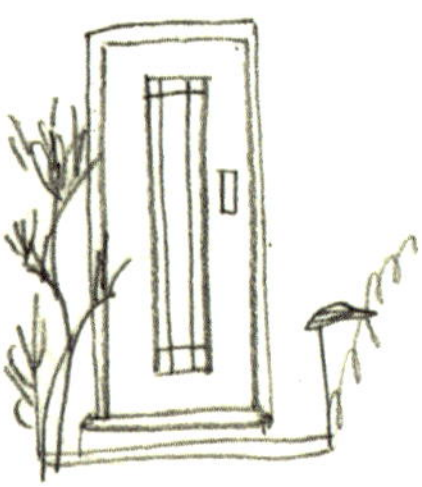

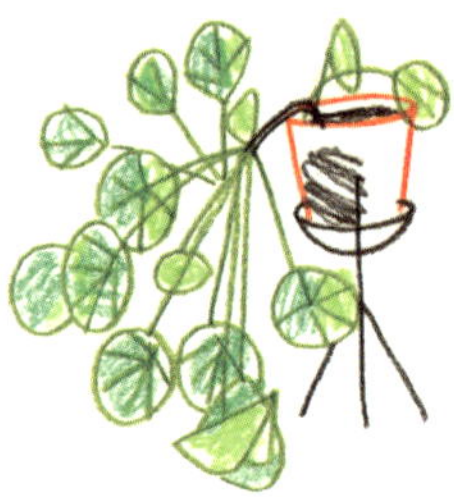

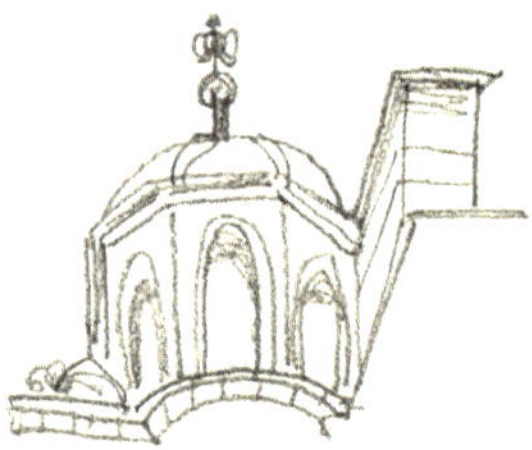

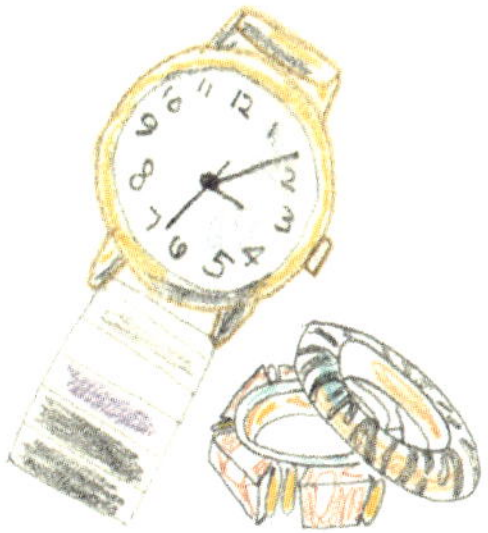

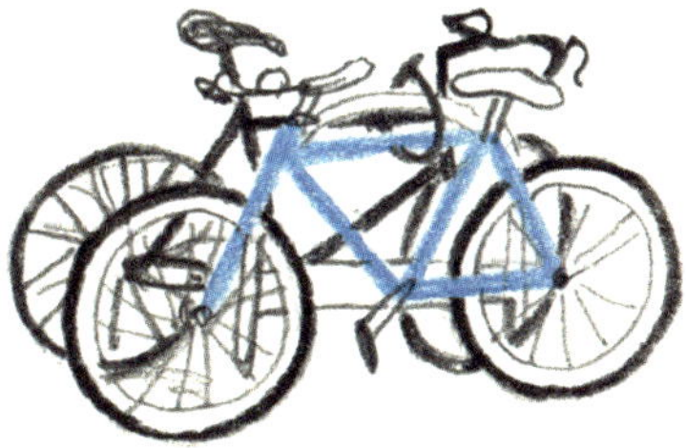

Draw with purpose

I like my drawings to say something, and to be easily "read." With a drawing, you can tell complex stories that will be understood in an instant, without the use of words. I find mindful coloring a bit pointless and boring, and doodling a little inward looking (although I do enjoy it too). There is also no doubt that drawing has therapeutic value, another reason to do it. When you are thinking about how to draw a line or make a mark, you don't think about anything else. Even just doing a drawing that is a straightforward representation of the thing it's meant to be feels "good."

Draw more often

The more often you draw, the better your drawings will become. If you draw often enough, it will start to feel like writing. Look more at the subject of your drawing than at your drawing itself, and draw it again and again.

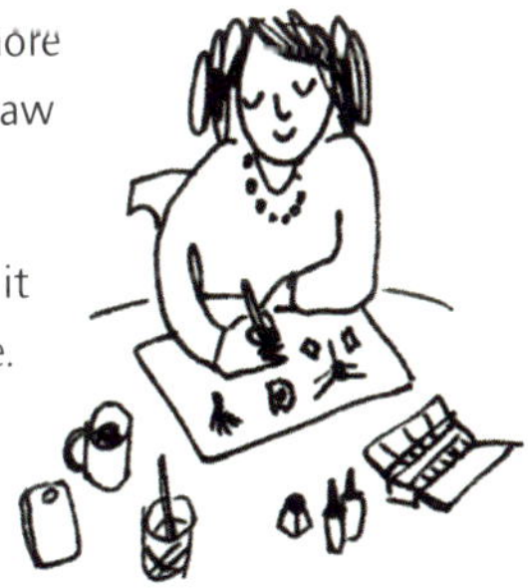

Making the first mark is difficult if you're worrying about "doing it wrong." It's important not to worry about what a drawing looks like. "Wrong" drawings are just as precious as the well-observed drawings that you'll do after plenty of practice. Looking at them all together when you've completed the journal, you will see that the progression you have made is beautiful too.

How to use this journal

This diary is divided into sections, each focusing on a set of details or objects, depending on what's around at that time of year. You can draw in your diary and collect four drawings a day, every day, or if you prefer, draw in your journal a lot in one day and then revisit it after a while to complete it. You can start in the beginning or in the middle. This diary is meant to be a personal artifact that will grow with you, depending on what your daily life is like—how you use it is up to you.

You don't really need a specific working routine. I just draw as often as I can, wherever I can—sitting at the kitchen table late at night when no one will ask me to do anything else, or whenever there's time to spare during the day. "Small things" are particularly well suited as subject matter for this style of working.

You will see more of an improvement in your drawings if you draw often. The more you draw, the more you will start to understand what things really look like, and how they fit together, which makes it all easier to re-create the next time you try.

You probably won't feel as much pressure about doing a "good" drawing if you're producing plenty of them all the time. The more time you dedicate to drawing, the more you will discover ways of drawing that you enjoy, and different marks and materials that work for you. Using this journal as a guide, you can become more experimental with your subjects and methods as your confidence grows.

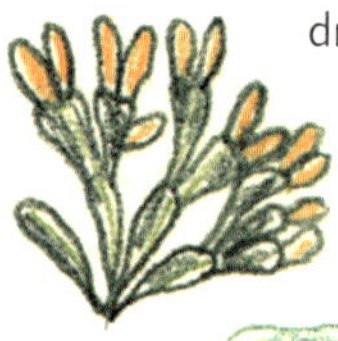

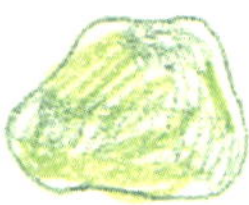

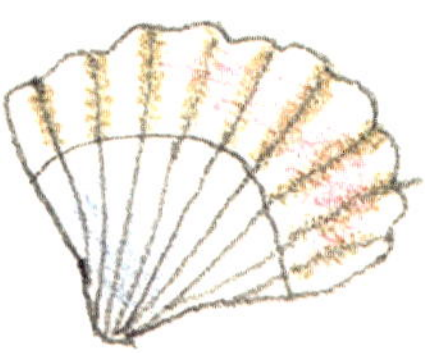

There isn't really an end point with drawing; there is always room to improve and develop, however skilled you become. I noticed my own drawings improving as I worked on this journal. Likewise, there are always more beautiful, inspiring, interesting things to look at and represent. Drawing something can lead you somewhere else.

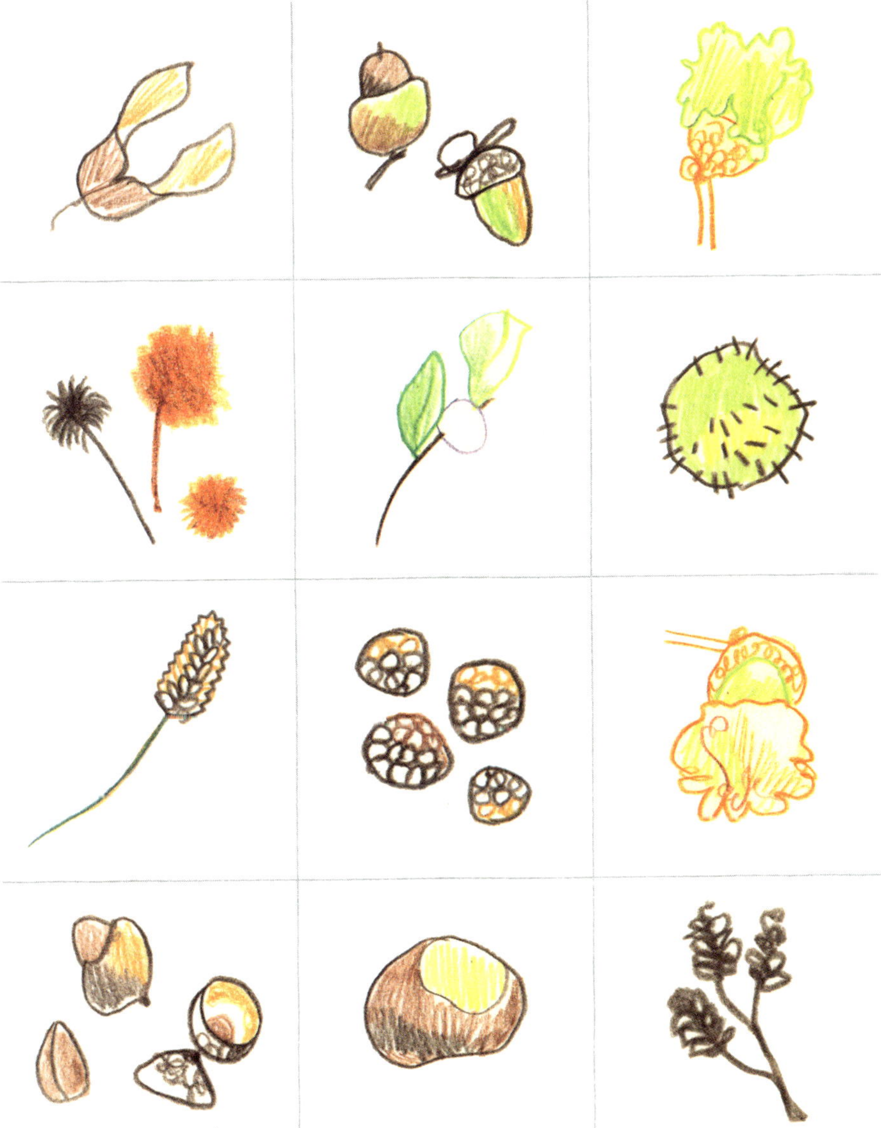

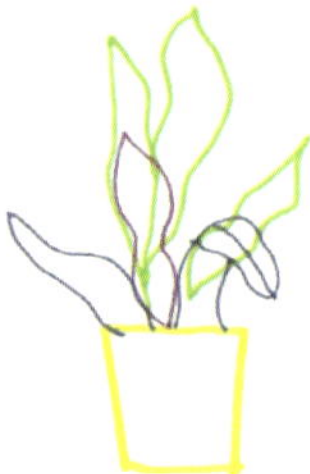
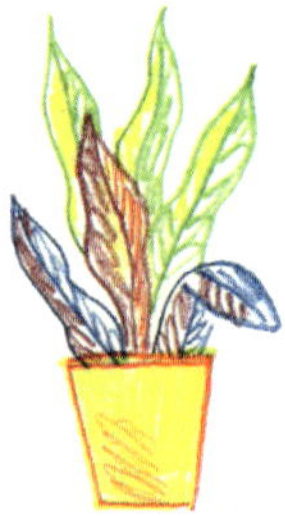
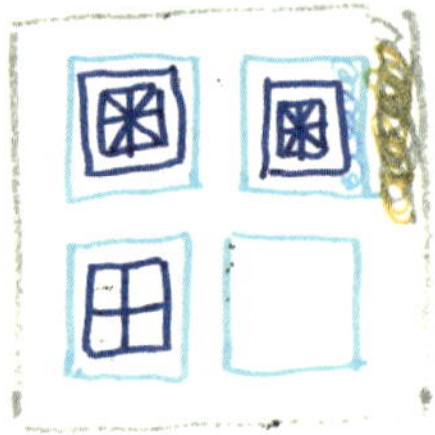
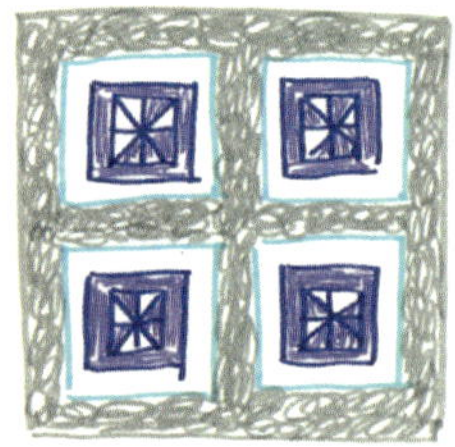

What's the grid for?

The grid acts as a way of framing things. I might suggest subjects to draw that seem quite abstract, such as pipe joints, but together they will make an interesting collection.

Fill each grid with drawings of the suggested thing. If finding thirty-six different examples is too difficult, draw the same thing more than once in different ways, from different angles or using different materials, or ask people to send you pictures of new things to draw.

If a drawing of something comes out strange, instead of erasing it, try drawing it again in a different box. Compare the two drawings: Which one looks better? What is it about that drawing that makes it more successful? What can you learn from the comparison that will help you in another drawing? As you fill up each grid, you'll be able to see your observation skills develop and change throughout the journal, which will make a satisfying record of your progress.

WHY DRAW?

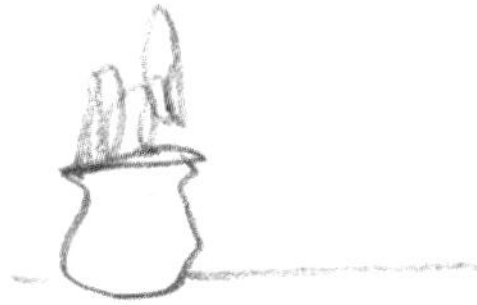

Why not simply take a photo? For me, drawing isn't just about realism. A simple drawing may tell a story more clearly than a realistic one because it only includes the essential visual information needed in order to communicate, and leaves out the rest.

Each new drawing is a surprise, you never quite know how it will come out; it's like putting what you see through a "you filter." Your mood, the circumstances you are in when you do a drawing, your location, will all affect how a drawing turns out, and that's what makes it interesting. It's also a fun experiment; how do different materials set each other off on a page? What can you do with different marks? There are endless combinations of colors and techniques and endless things to look at and draw.

Why draw? I don't know—I just need to do it! I like to put what I see under the closest scrutiny, to try to nail it to the page and make it mine.

Draw what you want to remember: something that simply looks nice, or that warrants recording for other reasons. It's more probable that you'll remember something if you spend a while looking at it.

I love noticing something that would make a great drawing, and imagining what I'd use to draw it, how I would capture its character. With a drawing, you can edit or exaggerate in a way that you can't with a photo. You can leave things out and draw only what you want to draw. There will be "truth" in your choices, even if your drawing doesn't look realistic.

Perfect realism in a drawing takes too long for me. There is so much to take in. The world changes quickly, I want to get as much of it down as possible while I have the chance.

The purpose of drawing

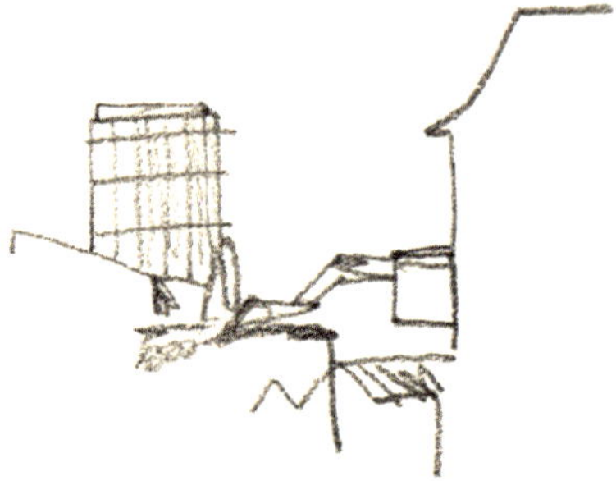

Drawing can link your inner self to the outside world. Your drawings don't need to describe an opinion or even a coherent thought, just present observations. A coherent thought or opinion may emerge from a collection of drawings, even if it wasn't clear to you when you started out. You are working out your ideas via a practical process.

During turbulent times, drawing can feel pointless or even indulgent. There are always more worthwhile things you can be doing. But in those moments when you aren't working, helping others, or just getting on with living, it is a valuable practice. Why? Even if your drawings aren't directly about the state of the world, your viewpoint will be clear. What will you choose to include in your drawings? How will you capture the world as it changes? Will you make comparisons or show contrasts?

Your drawings don't always have to be of a subject you like; you might use a drawing to make a critical comment on something you think needs to be brought to our attention, such as beautiful run-down buildings that have been left to decay, or luxury apartments that have been built carelessly where local communities used to thrive.

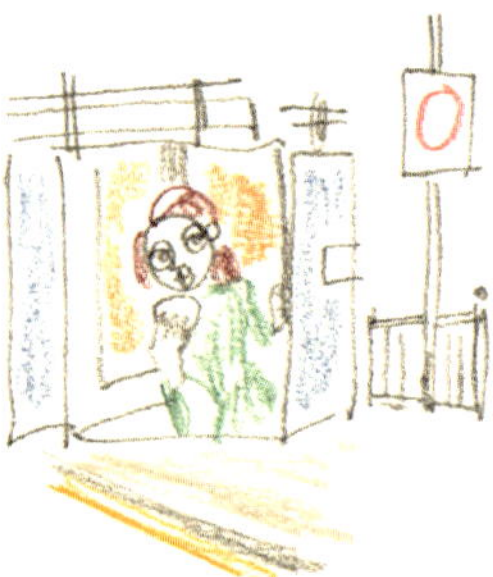

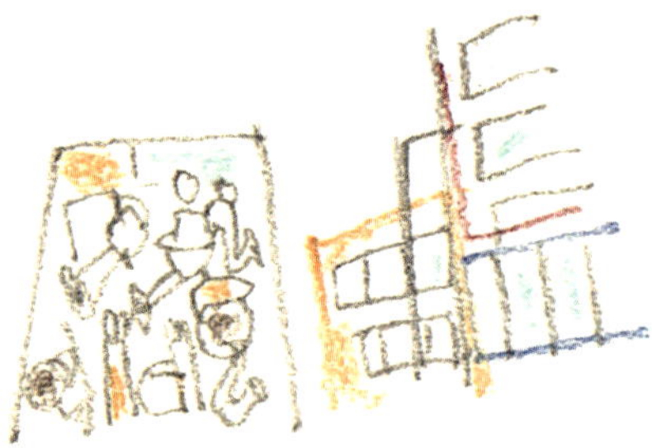

WHY SMALL DRAWINGS?

I take my students out drawing regularly. With a group of beginners, when they sit down to begin a drawing, there are things that prevent them from starting. Choosing what to draw is difficult, the level of detail is overwhelming, they want to do a really good drawing, and there's so much pressure that they can't do anything. They start with a minute piece of detail in the middle of a huge page and are unable to take in the whole scene. I tried to think of something that would help them get past this point, something to get them started that they wouldn't feel anxious about.

I asked them to divide their page into postage stamp–sized rectangles, and then gave them one hour to fill up all the rectangles with tiny studies of the area. They could look at architectural details, people, natural forms, or any objects that caught their eye. They were very happy to do this.

There wasn't the same pressure as there would have been if I'd asked them to do one large drawing. If a drawing went wrong, they could just start another. Because the drawings were tiny, they'd been forced to simplify. They couldn't possibly include every detail in a drawing the size of a postage stamp. Together, all the small drawings made one big, beautiful fragmented drawing.

As with this journal, the smallness of the drawings makes doing them easier. You can do them quickly wherever you are. You can be discreet if you want to be—it won't necessarily be obvious to anyone else that you are drawing.

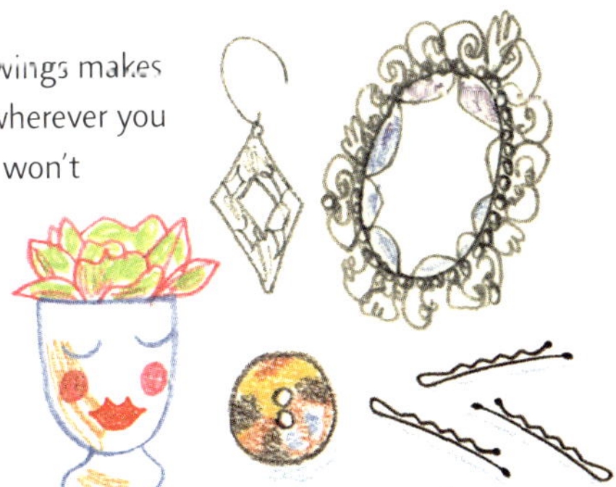

DRAWING FROM PHOTOS OR FROM REAL LIFE

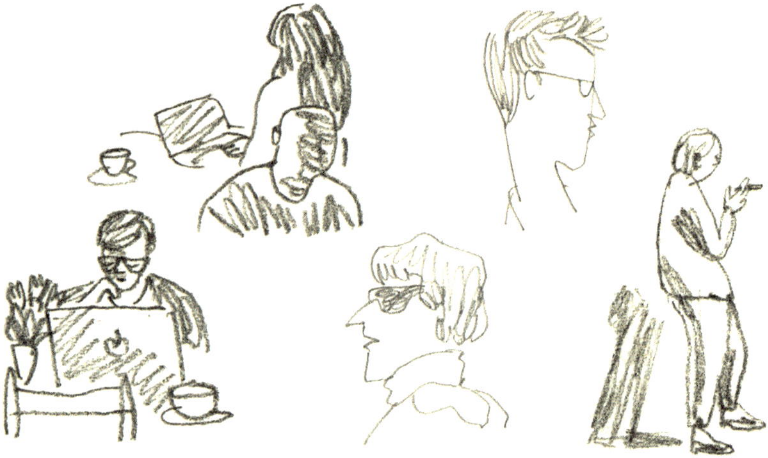

I think there is value in drawing both from life and also from photographs. If you draw from a photo, you have no time limit, you can look for as long as you want, you can draw places or things you might not be able to get to or see otherwise. If you simply want to show what something looks like, drawing from a photo can be ideal. The drawing can still be interesting, depending on what you say with it, what you use it for, and the marks you use to make it.

But there is something particularly exhilarating about drawing from life. When you manage to capture something as it changes, to pin it down, or create a meaningful likeness, it feels like magic. What's happening around you will affect your drawing; what you notice will be different from what you might notice when you look at a photograph.

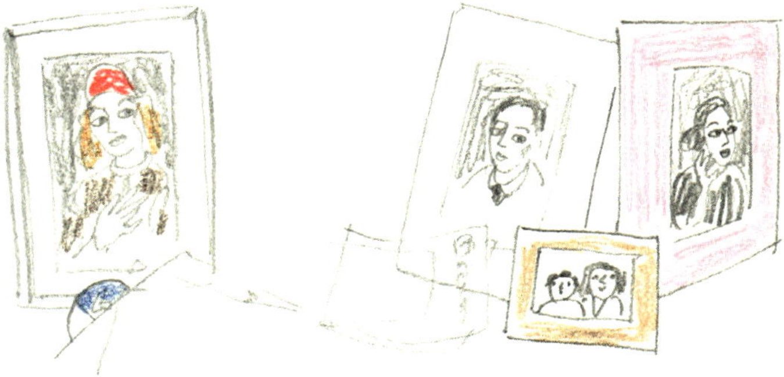

Light behaves differently in real life; colors look richer and more varied, your field of view isn't cropped by a square or rectangular frame.

When drawing from life, your subject might move or change before you've finished drawing. Unfinished drawings can also be interesting; they show what seemed important to draw first, the essence of that thing.

If you think your subject won't be still for very long, before you start, think about how it can be drawn with only a few marks. If you have only a limited amount of time to capture something as a whole, what are the most important parts to include?

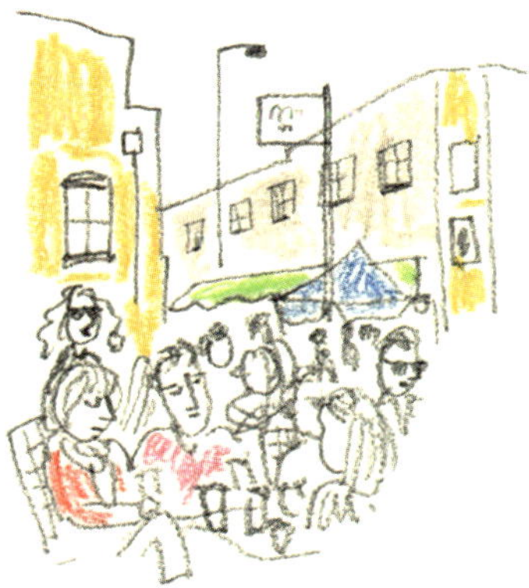

If there's something you want to draw but aren't able to at the time, photograph it to draw later. If there are places you can't get to that you'd like to draw, use the Internet to find a virtual scene.

STARTING A DRAWING

When you start any drawing, you have several choices to make: what to draw, which materials to use, and what to include in your picture. The weekly suggestions are there to help with this.

Choosing what to draw

When you look at anything before you start drawing it (a view, an object, a person), notice how many different qualities make it what it is (color, light, texture, shadow), as well as line and detail. What stands out the most to you about it? It might not be a line. Starting with a patch of color or texture, rather than with an outline, gives you more leeway when thinking about where any details need to go. If you've already put some basic shapes down, it's easier to place more definite marks.

I have suggested ways to simplify that visual information in your drawings. As you look, try to see the subject of your drawing as a collection of abstract shapes. By seeing it in this way, you remove it from what you know it to be, which will help you to draw what it really looks like rather than what you think it ought to look like.

Some of the things I've suggested for you to draw might not seem very picturesque. I think those things are just as interesting as more typically beautiful objects or scenes. I try not to be sentimental when I'm drawing; I like to show what's really there. Tangles of cords and extractor fans are as much a part of our lives as skylines and fall leaves and can be just as satisfying to draw.

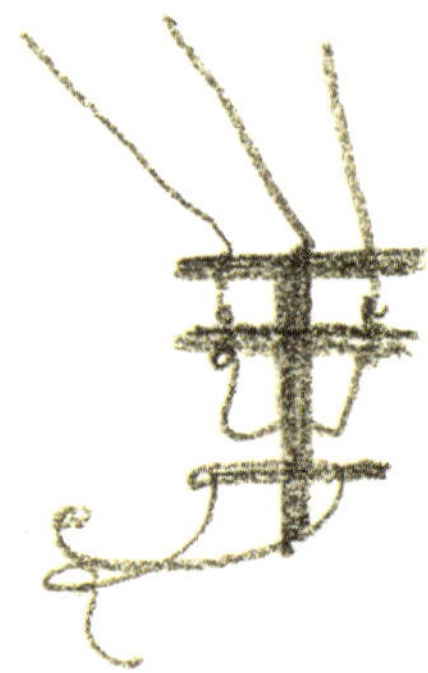

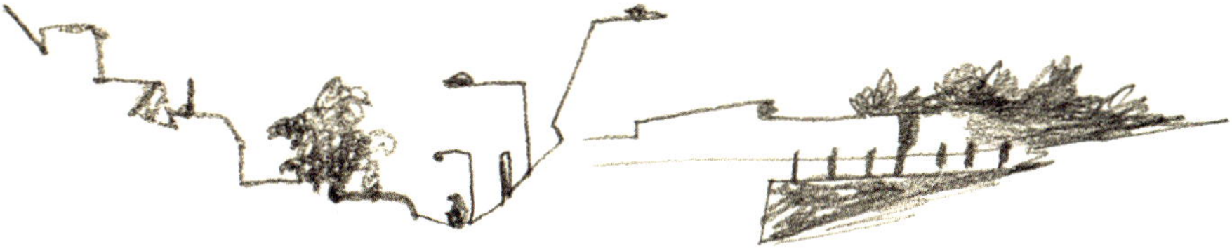

Choosing how to draw

As you draw more, you'll start to become aware of why you might use each material, and of which aspect of an object you want to capture.

You might find that your drawings work better if you purposefully don't try to make them look realistic. Instead, you can think of it as simply jotting down basic visual notes. Try to limit your materials to simplify the process.

You can "warm up" by doing some drawings or doodles on different sheets of paper. If you like any of your warm-up drawings, you can cut them out and paste them in your journal.

For more complicated objects, I sometimes drew the basic shapes with a fine, sharp pencil, then I drew over the top with color and erased the pencil lines. You may find this helpful but if not, just skip that stage. I think my drawings were actually better when I didn't bother doing that first. They look more spontaneous.

Because you'll be working with a lot of different materials, your style will probably change throughout the journal. That's a good thing. Don't worry about finding your own style too much, just continue observing, enjoying whatever comes out on the page. You might like some ways of working more than others. As you go through the journal, remember which techniques you have enjoyed and use those more often.

Don't worry about keeping your journal clean. Add your own notes about each thing if you want to, do extra doodles, test colors out in the margins, or down the edges of each page. It will be interesting to look back and see your thought processes and observations.

EMBRACING IMPERFECTION

Think before you reach for the eraser

Try not to worry about making a perfect line or drawing. If a line "goes wrong," it's tempting to erase it, but avoid using an eraser too much. Mistakes can be useful; keeping a "wrong" mark on your page makes it easier to see where a mark that looks better should go. In defense of inaccurate marks, they can have great character or tell you something else about what was going on at the time of drawing, as well as just what the thing looks like.

A mark may also look "wrong" until it becomes part of the whole drawing. Instead of erasing away inaccurate lines, keep adding and adjusting.

The more closely you observe what you're drawing, the more accurate and meaningful your lines will be, and the less need you'll have for an eraser.

If you find yourself using an eraser a lot and it's stopping you from drawing anything at all, use a pen instead.

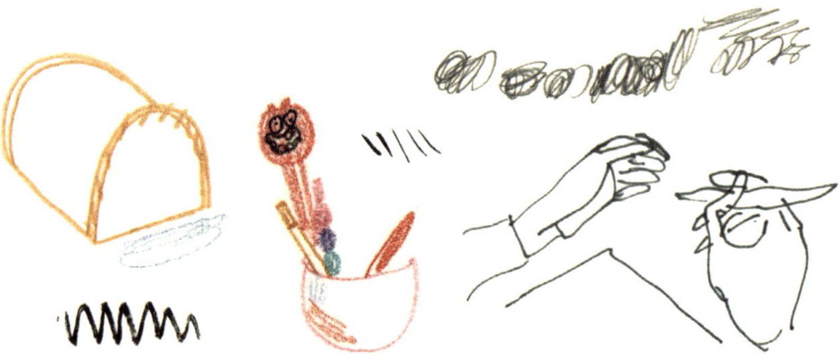

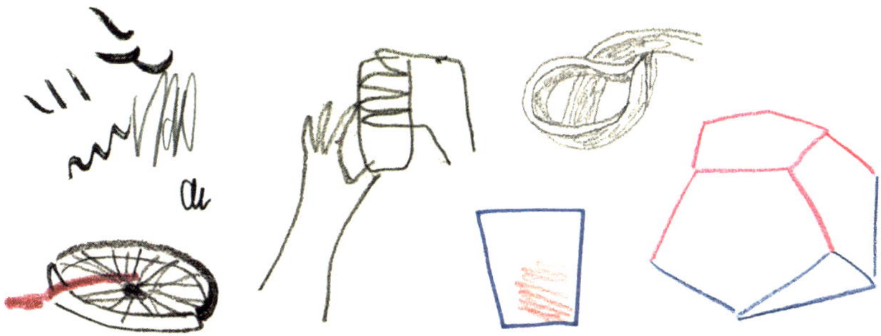

Being "good" at drawing and able to represent something in a realistic way may seem like a magical skill, but anyone can learn how to look closely, to compare distances, angles, proportions, colors, tones, textures, and atmosphere before they make a mark. The exciting and creative part is choosing what you do with those skills—what do you choose to represent and why? What can your drawings tell other people about the world and the way that you see it?

Remember that in this journal I've only included the drawings of mine that turned out well, there are many I didn't choose that looked completely wrong.

If you get stuck

If you find that starting a drawing is difficult, try doing it as a "blind drawing" (draw without looking at your drawing, only look at the thing you are drawing). Your drawings will probably look quite weird but that's OK, you'll be able to see places within the marks where you have closely observed what's there. Then draw in almost the same way, looking at your drawing a bit as you work, but looking mostly at the thing you are drawing. When you look at your drawing, don't correct yourself too much; just keep looking at the thing instead.

Another useful exercise is to try drawing with your "wrong" hand. That way you'll find that you draw more slowly, and concentrate harder on the marks because they're more difficult to make.

MATERIALS

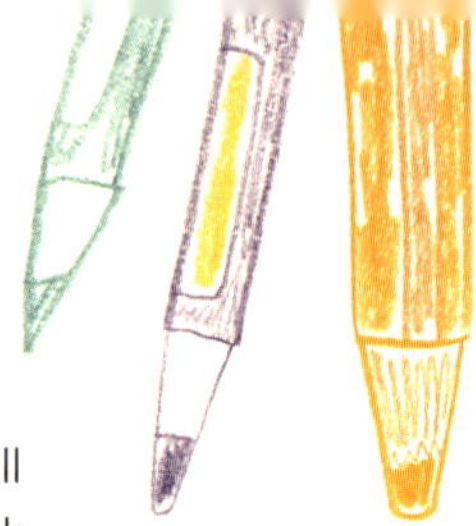

I have suggested using standard materials that you'll find in any art store. If you can, go to a store and try out materials on the corners of pages in this journal rather than buying online. You'll find that different brands' products create marks of different quality and texture. Choose a selection that you like. Usually, the more expensive the product, the brighter and more long-lasting the color will be. Inexpensive products are fine to use too.

I've found that it makes things easier if I keep my materials organized in separate, clear pencil cases—pens in one, pencils in another, crayons in another—so I can easily find what I need.

Your choice of materials should depend on what type of drawing you want to do. A fine liner can be the right tool for a stylized illustration or symbol that tells us clearly what the thing is. If you want to create a representation that includes a wider range of visual qualities, a broader "truth"—light, color, or texture—other materials can do this better.

You may want to have elements of both of those things, "truth" and "simplification," in a drawing. What is the point of the drawing—is it to remember? Or just to experiment and see how you can represent that thing in different ways?

Colored pencils

Wax-type or nonsoluble colored pencils are waterproof and smudge-proof. If you sharpen them, you can make finely detailed marks. As the point wears down, you can use them to make thicker marks or patches of texture. I used mid-range, oil-based colored pencils to do the drawings in this journal.

Graphite pencils

Pencils come in varying degrees of hardness. If a pencil lead is soft, more graphite will come off on the paper when you use it than if the pencil lead is hard. Soft pencils make darker, smudgier marks than hard pencils, which make fine, light marks. You can sharpen a soft pencil to make fine marks with it, but it will wear down more quickly than a hard pencil.

I like using a very sharp, soft pencil to make dark, clearly defined marks, then shade with it as it wears down. It means I end up sharpening pencils a lot.

I have a selection of three or four pencils: hard, medium, and soft—you don't really need a whole set.

Pencil sharpener

This is an essential item. Get one that collects your pencil shavings to avoid getting pencil dust all over everything.

Erasers

Putty erasers are good for big drawings, if you're working back into layers of graphite or charcoal, but they aren't very precise if you're working on a small scale. Retractable erasers that look like pens are more suitable, as are the type that are "dust free," because they don't leave crumbs of eraser all over your page.

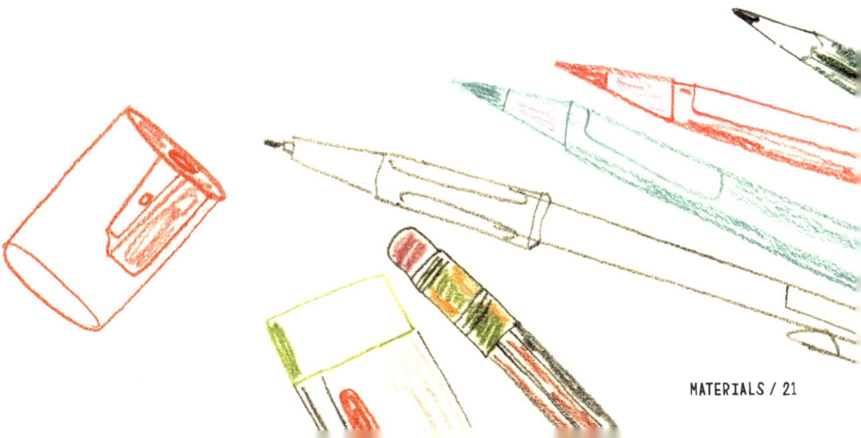

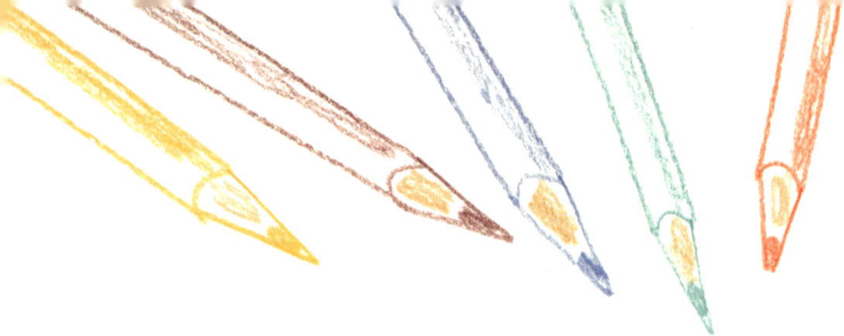

Watercolor pencils

These are colored pencils to which you can add water, to make the pencil marks turn into a painted texture. They make chalkier marks than other colored pencils.

I haven't used them in this book, because, strictly speaking, using color washes is painting rather than drawing, but during the year you may feel like trying something a little different. If you do experiment with watercolor pencils, don't be tempted to turn all your closely observed marks into color wash—use sparingly and leave some areas of definition so you can see what's what, or wait for the water to dry and work back over the top with more pencil marks.

Personally, if I'm out drawing, I like to be able to hold a few pencils in one hand while I draw quickly with the other. Using a jar of water and a brush and waiting around for water to dry doesn't fit with this technique.

Graphite sticks

Graphite sticks are great for working on larger drawings; they make thicker marks than smaller pencils. I've used them in this journal in a couple of places, when I wanted really broad, crumbly soft lines. I like the kind that are inside a plastic casing so my hand doesn't get too dirty when I use them.

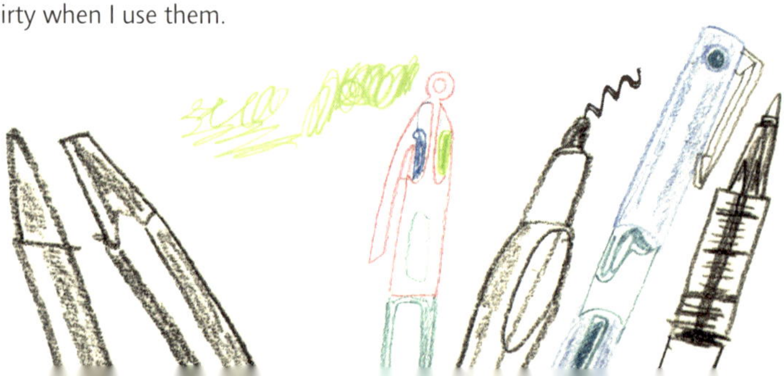

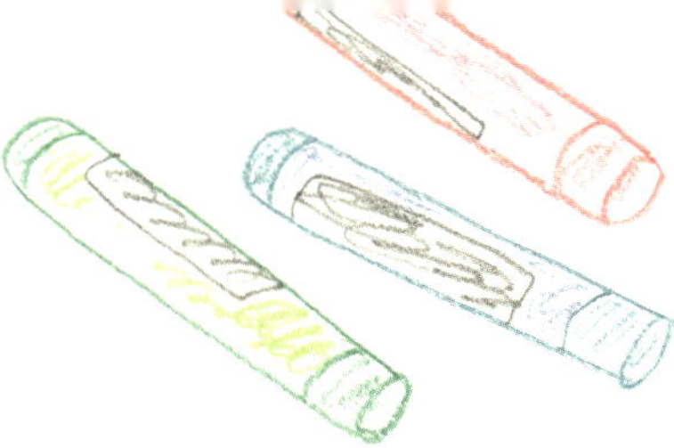

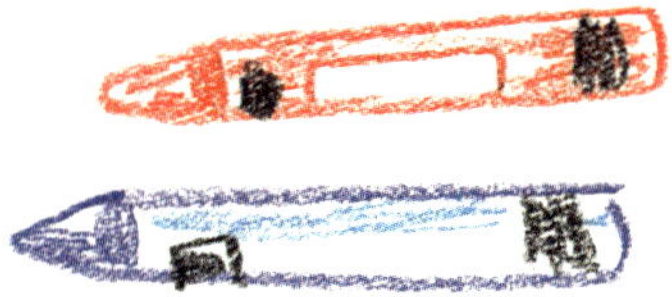

Wax crayons & pastels

These are good for patches of soft color or broad lines. Instead of buying a whole set, you can choose a small selection of colors. As with colored pencils, there's a huge variety available, all made for different drawing techniques. I like quite hard, waxy crayons that don't smudge too much and look bright on the page; you can also draw over them easily with other materials. Chalk and oil pastel will rub off and smudge; I think they work better for larger drawings. Try some out and see what suits you.

Colored marker pens

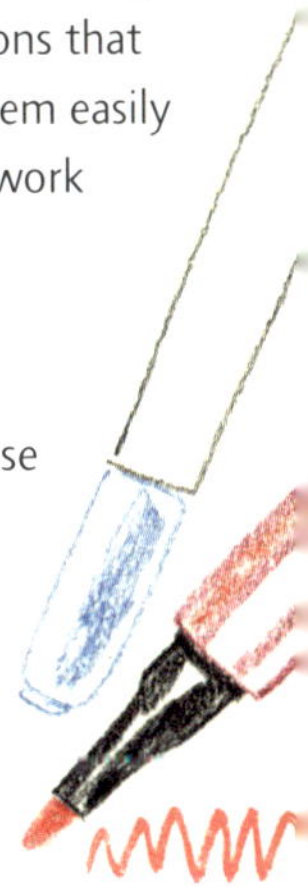

I've bought loads of those expensive markers, but I never really use them, because they're too big to carry around easily. Inexpensive markers work fine. Try all of the different types available. I like pens with soft-ish tips, so I can make fine lines as well as even patches of color. Coloring in with finer pens will give you a scratchy texture; brush-tip pens will give you a flat, even texture. Dried-out pens can make interesting marks too.

Fine liners & ballpoint pens

Fine liners vary too. Try them all. Ballpoint pens or cartridge pens will give you more variation in line quality than super-fine technical pens.

A fine liner might seem like the obvious choice of pen for a drawing. It's probably the pen you're most likely to have on you, and the lines they make are consistent, giving you good control. But consider which aspect of your subject you want to capture. Is it simply the outline?

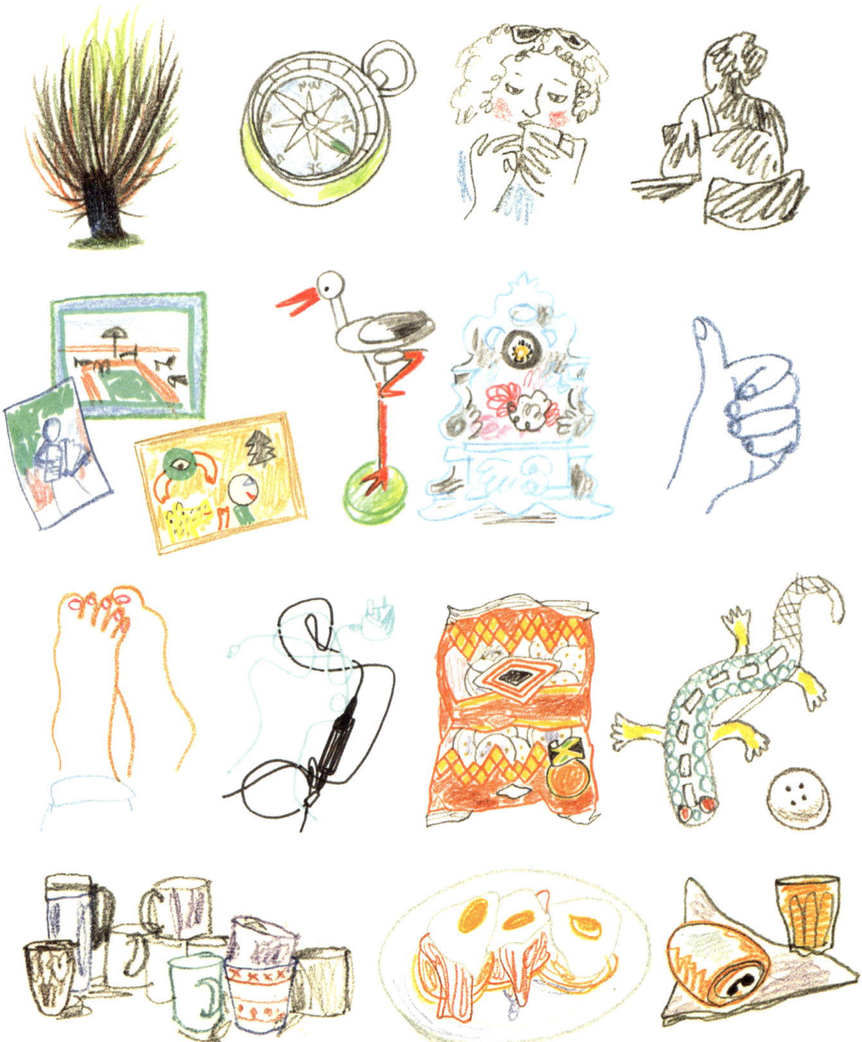

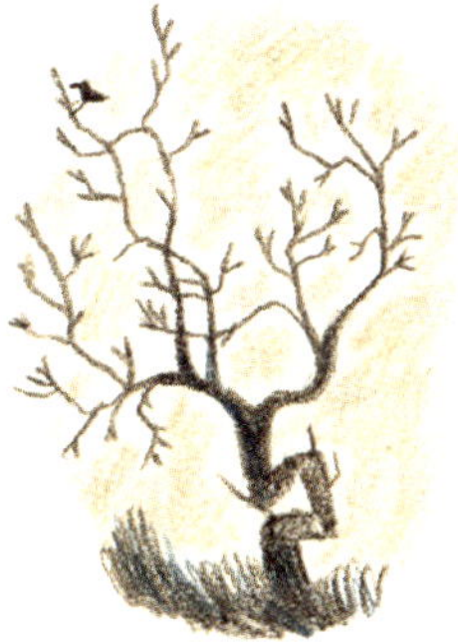

Winter

If it's too cold to draw outdoors, have a look at the huge variety of things in your house that you could draw: knickknacks, pictures on the walls, and stuff of all shapes and sizes in your junk drawer. Open up a cabinet, draw whatever is inside, and appreciate the coziness of these familiar items. Alternatively, you can venture outdoors and do some quick sketches of bare trees, then go back into the warmth.

BARE OR EVERGREEN TREES

Whether in city parks, a yard, or the countryside, trees are ideal subjects for drawing. Without their leaves, winter trees seem suddenly expressive—bare trunks and branches clearly visible, twisting against the sky. Trees that have had their branches cut right back to keep them healthy can look like gnarled old hands. New shoots spray out of the stumps, perfect for quick pencil marks. You might notice trees with ivy growing up their trunks in cloudy shapes, and trees sprouting from other trees. What color is the sky around the branches?

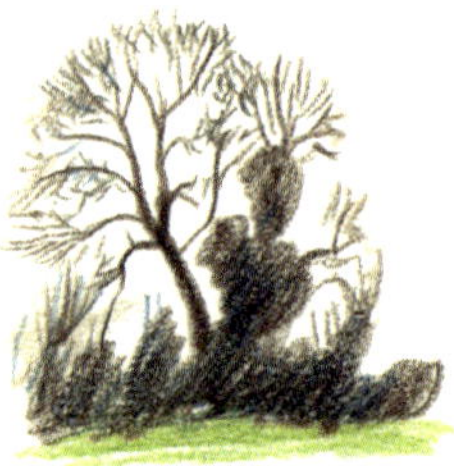

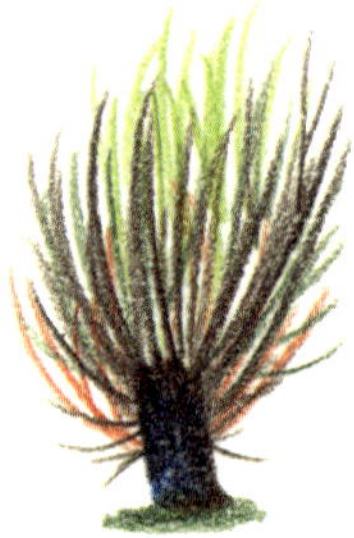

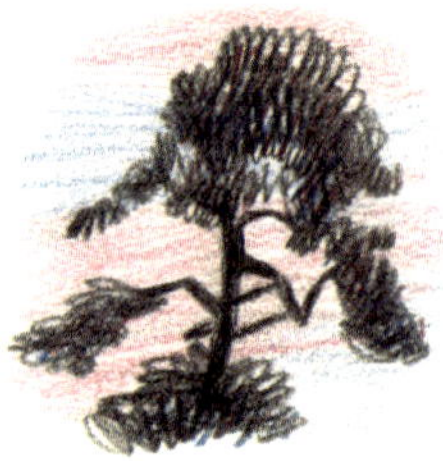

Using colored pencils, try layering several dark colors on top of each other to make a rich black. Press quite hard when drawing the trunk and branches, then use a lighter pressure and finer lines to draw the twigs nearest the sky. For evergreen trees, look for the shape formed by the leaves and the different colors created by light and shade.

JUNK DRAWER

Most of us have a collection of junk—things we keep but don't display. Here, you will find objects of various shapes, some quite complicated. The rubber finger monster's arm is hanging on by a thread—I should throw it away. I like the way someone has designed a little flower and boat for these child's nail clippers. Look for interesting details. Which objects would you choose to draw?

I drew these with colored pencils, using the sharp point for details and the side of the tip for softer colored patches. Even though the monster is blue, it reflected a purple light in those brighter patches. I drew the shadow on the pawn using a color opposite to the one on the pawn itself, cool blue on warm beige. The circular shapes at the base didn't come out perfectly, but I don't think it matters.

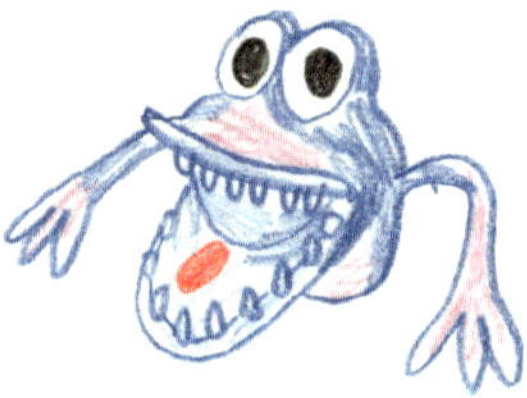

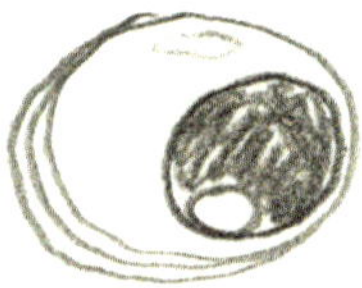

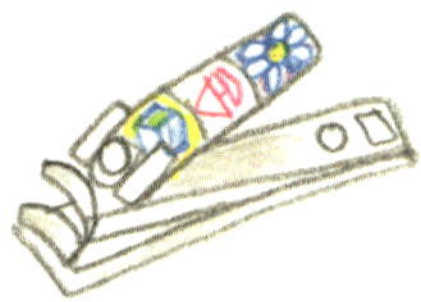

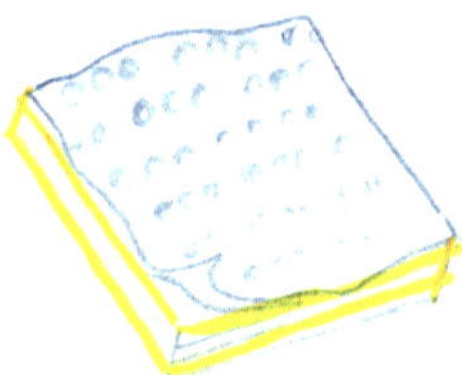

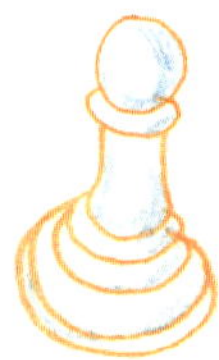

PEOPLE LOOKING AT THEIR PHONES

People looking at phones are everywhere: friends, family, commuters, and just bystanders. Because they are occupied, they might remain still, and so they probably won't notice you drawing them. What is the shape of their hair? How much of their face is visible? Is it masked by their hand and phone? Do scarves or collars hide their chin? How long are their fingers in relation to the phone, and how are they holding it?

You can draw people from the front or side, sitting or lying down, or ignore the phone and hands and just draw the face. I used a soft (4B) pencil, graphite stick, and crayon; I wanted something that I could make soft marks with as I worked out what went where.

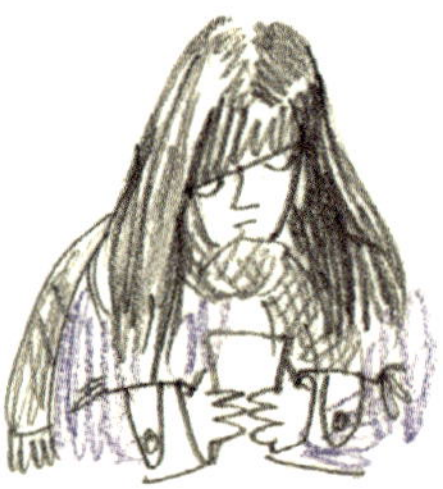
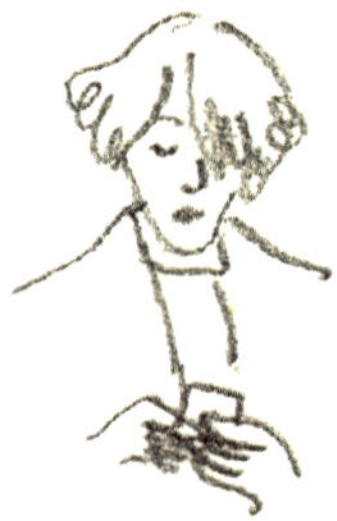
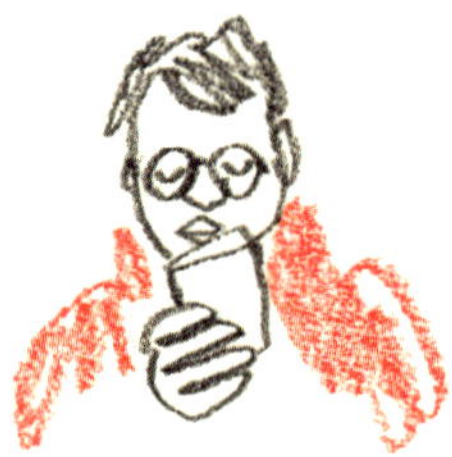
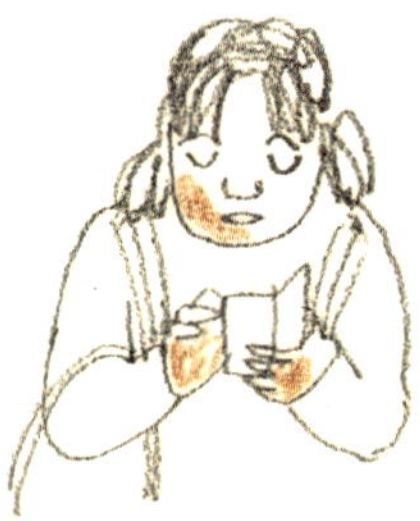
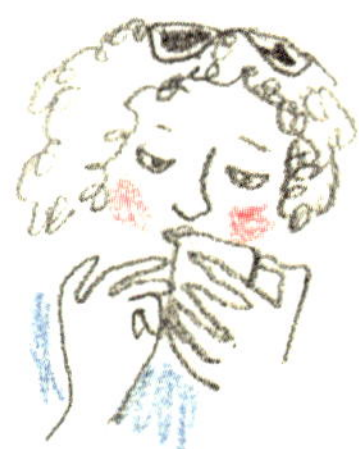
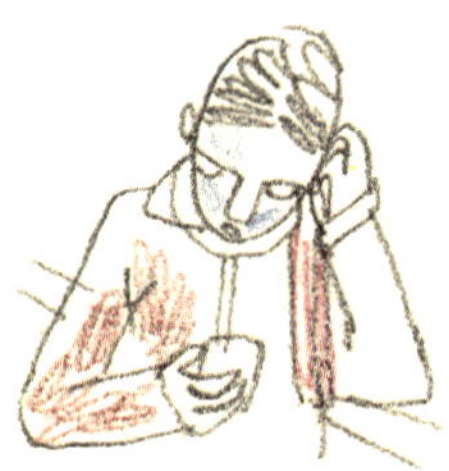

PEOPLE ON LAPTOPS

People absorbed in work on a laptop will be unselfconscious, in natural poses. Look for them in well-lit coffee shops or libraries—are they near a window? Which part of them is in shade? Look at their posture—are they slumping over? Where is their head in relation to their body? Not usually perched right on the top but hanging forward. What shape are their shoulders—rounded or square? Are they balancing their laptop on their knees? Is there anything on the table?

Using a soft graphite stick, I started by drawing the laptop—an easier shape than the person, and it is useful for measuring the size of their figure against it. I then worked outward from the laptop, adding shadow as I went with loose, sketchy marks. Try simplifying shapes, such as the shoulders, with one soft line.

PICTURES

Drawing someone else's work is a worthwhile exercise. Draw any pictures that you have on your walls—paintings, photographs, children's drawings, postcards, posters, or calendars. If you're drawing a painting, as you look closely at each part of the picture, you will form an understanding of how the artist made it—which colors they used and in what order they put the image together.

I didn't attempt to make exact copies of each picture; I drew simplified thumbnails. The colors are approximate. As you draw, try to think about which colors will work. When you use markers with colored pencil, as I have done here, the markers' colors "pop" into the foreground. Can you use that effect on the frame or in the pictures? I really enjoyed drawing these very different images with the same approach, so they all go together.

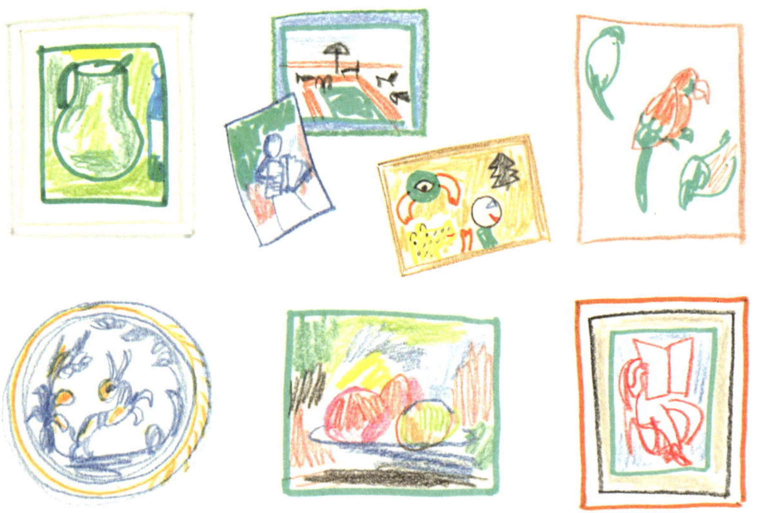

KNICKKNACKS

Do you have any favorite knickknacks, heirlooms, or souvenirs? I have a collection by my desk like a shrine. Yours might evoke memories of people or places, where you got them, who gave them to you, and what life was like at the time. You can write down those memories. I love the way precious objects hold stories. If you don't have many, search online or visit a junk store and photograph whatever catches your eye.

I bought the wooden heron from a junk store in Tallinn, Estonia. The storekeeper was behind the door pouring himself a shot of vodka. My mum dug up the china head of the little doll in the yard of the house we lived in when I was a child, then made the body to go with it. My friend tried to steal that cow-shaped milk jug, but I wouldn't let her.

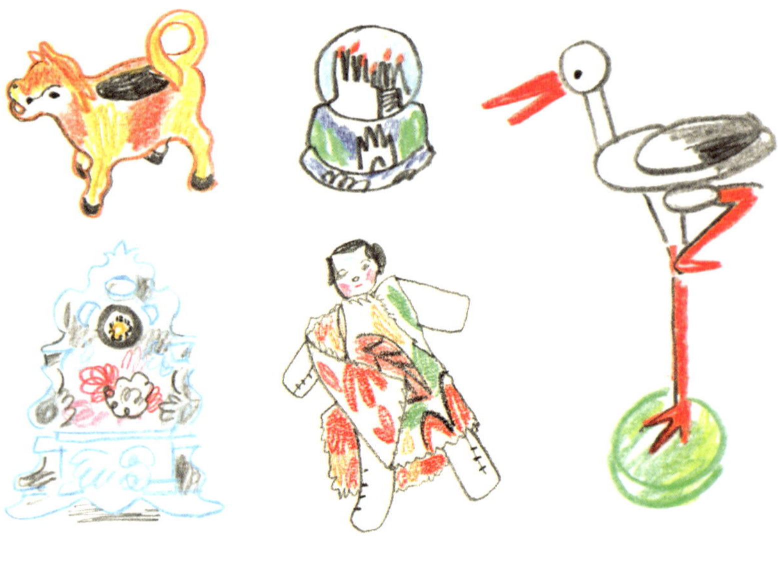

HANDS

Separated from the body, as they will be in these drawings, hands can look quite odd, almost like coral or sea anemones. Draw both hands, experimenting with different positions by making gestures and contorting them into other shapes. Try to draw what you really see, not what you think a hand looks like. Curled over, the ends of your fingers might look like kidney beans or peanuts. If you point at your nose and look at the tip of your finger, it looks like a circular blob. My palm is quite square. What shape is yours?

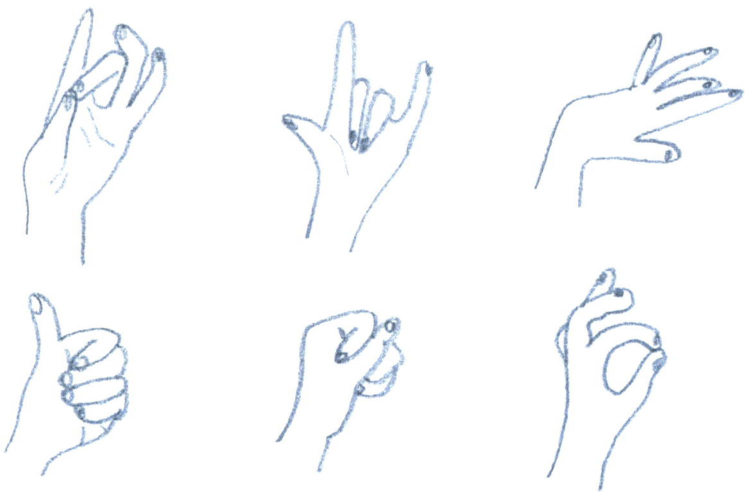

You can draw with colored pencils, or anything that lets you make clearly defined lines (good for drawing fingernails and wrinkles), such as a graphite pencil or pen. I haven't colored mine in, but you may prefer to—perhaps try making each hand a different color.

FEET

As with hands, feet are a great subject to use for drawing practice if you're feeling lazy, because you don't have to go anywhere to see them. I enjoyed drawing mine; they have a rather square shape with short toes—particularly the littlest toe, which seems ridiculously small.

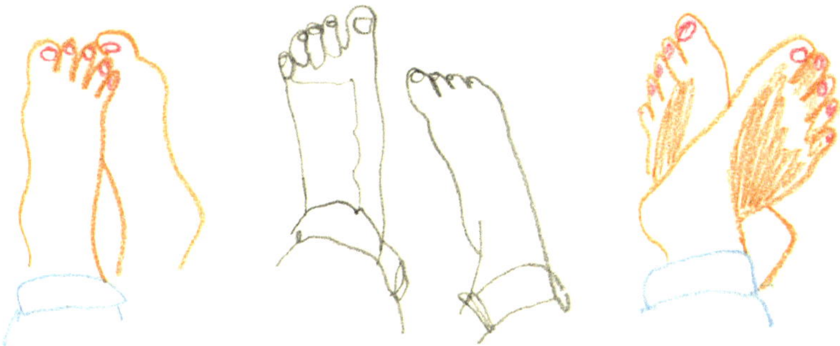

I used a graphite stick in the center drawing, because I wanted the soft but clearly defined lines you can get if you don't press very hard. I twisted it as I followed the edge of the shadow along the bottom of my toes, and down across my foot. I drew the other feet with a wax crayon, which is good for coloring patches of rough shadow. For the skin, I just used one color, but you could use two—one for the light side, one for the side that's in shadow, then different colors for your toenails or pants.

TANGLES OF CORDS

Most of us have countless devices to keep fully charged, and plug sockets surrounded by a mass of tangled-up wires. You can draw the same cords each day, and notice how they fall differently after you attach or disconnect something, or look around the house for different arrangements.

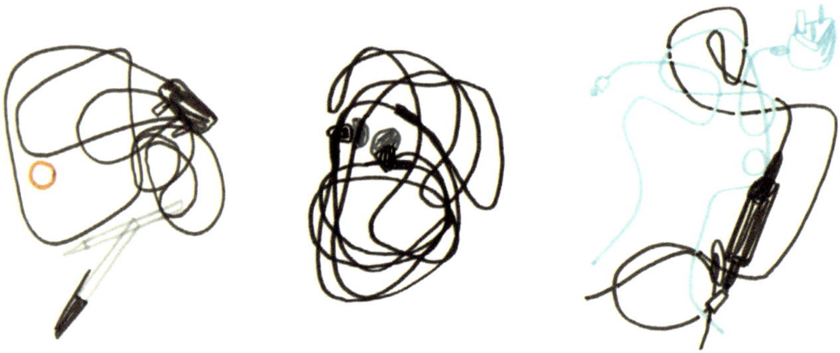

Are the cords in your house tangled and nightmarish, with other objects wound up in them too, or perfectly tied up? Either way, your collection of cords will reflect an element of your personality. Try using different colors for each cord for a more interesting arrangement.

FOOD PACKAGING

The packaging I already had in my kitchen seemed a little ordinary, so I went to the store "for research" and bought a lot of candy—in interesting packages, of course—and any other things that caught my eye. Have a look in your kitchen for packaging with appealing details such as bright colors, logos, and pictures.

You could choose a box or bag with a solid color, but if your packaging is clear or partly transparent, use paler colors to draw what's inside to make the product look like it's behind plastic.

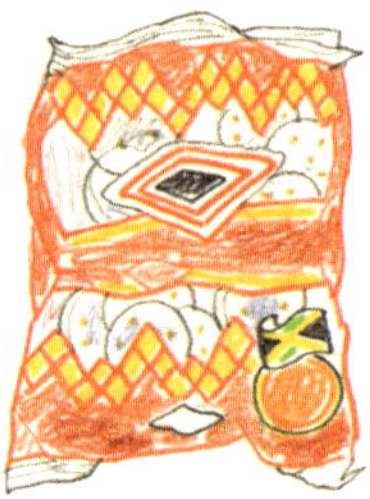
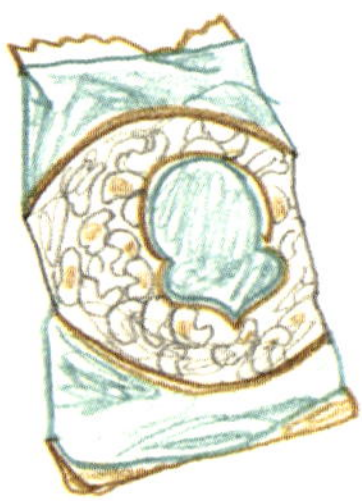
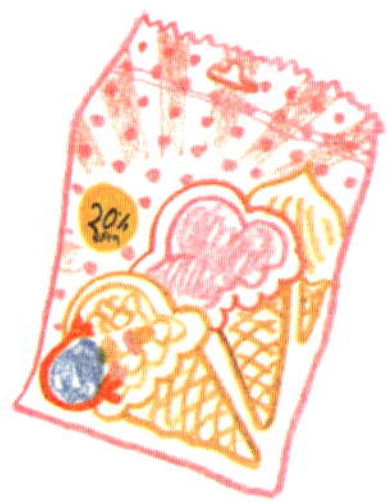
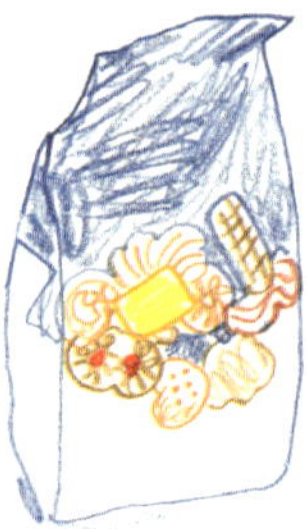
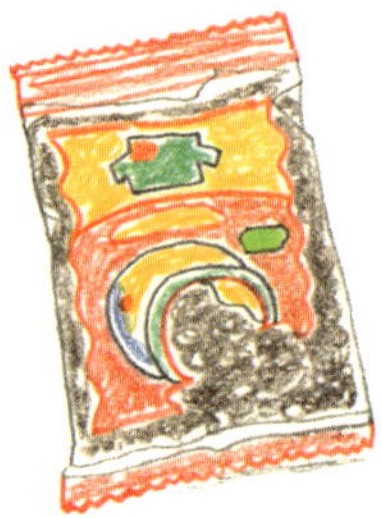
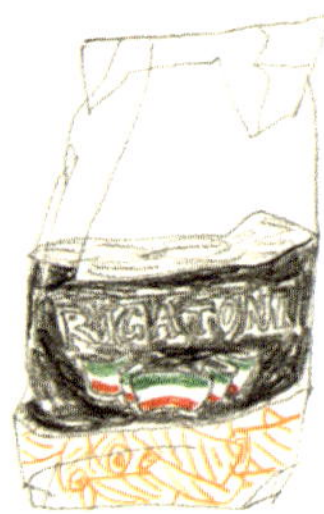

BROOCHES, BADGES & BUTTONS

Old sewing boxes can be full of bits and pieces that remind you of the past. I have a box of pretty buttons that I've never gotten around to sewing onto anything, various antique brooches that are too sharp to wear but too beautiful to throw away, and badges I collected as a child. If you still have similar items, what do they remind you of? If you don't have any, look online for collections of costume jewelry or pins.

You can start by drawing a single button or group a few colorful, intricate items together for a more challenging subject. Think about what color to use for any outline or detail, but resist the temptation to use black by default. What color is each different section?

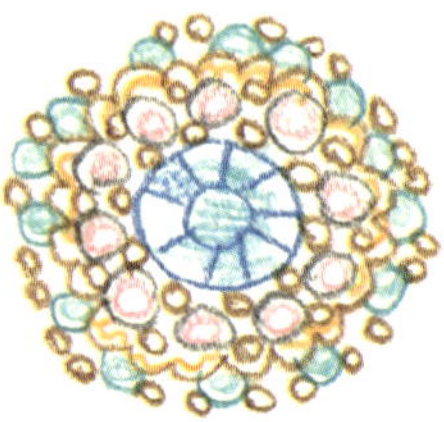

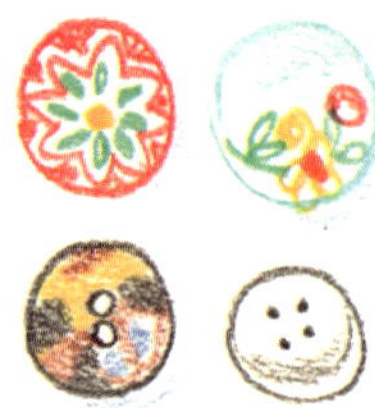
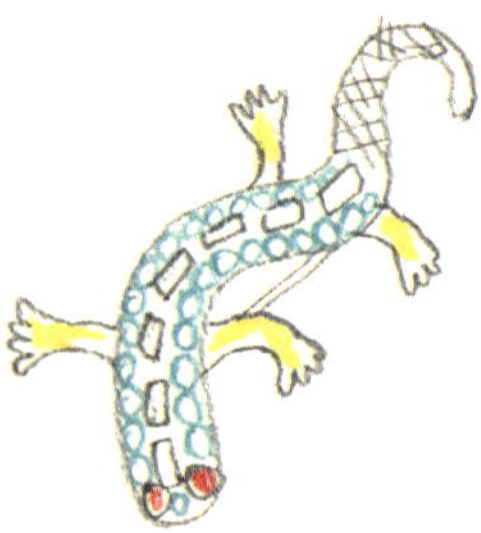
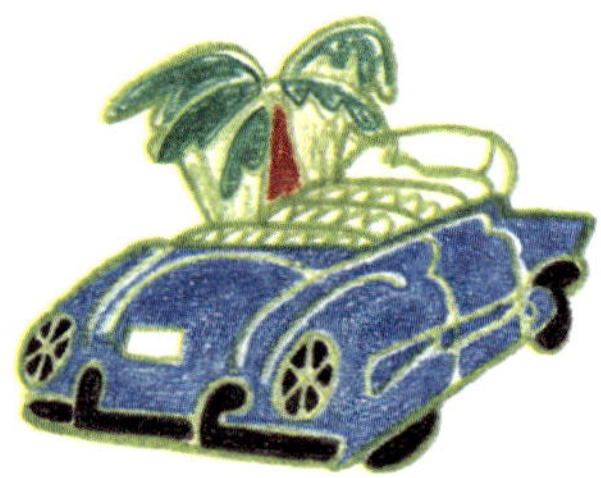
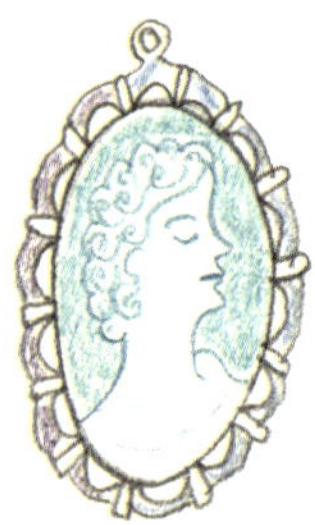

THINGS IN CABINETS

Are your cabinets clean and well ordered, or are there so many odds and ends crammed in that something falls out every time you open the door? Either way, whatever's inside will provide a variety of interesting shapes and colors for you to work with.

Using the outside of the cabinet as a frame, try to fill the whole of each box. If there are a lot of items in the cabinet, try to simplify by drawing everything almost like a doodle—don't worry too much about scale and proportion. It's fine if your drawings just look like a hodgepodge of stuff with the odd recognizable thing jumping out, such as a piece of decoration, or identifiable shape. Draw your own cabinets and shelves, or ask friends to send you photographs of theirs to draw.

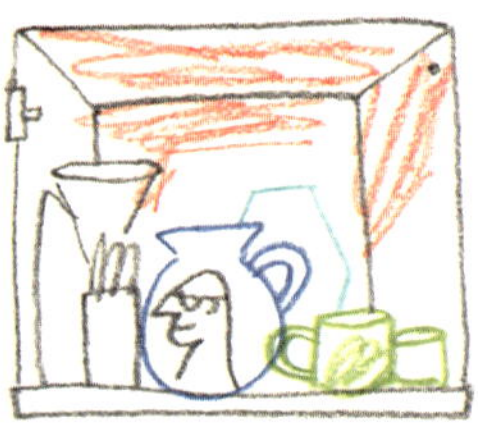
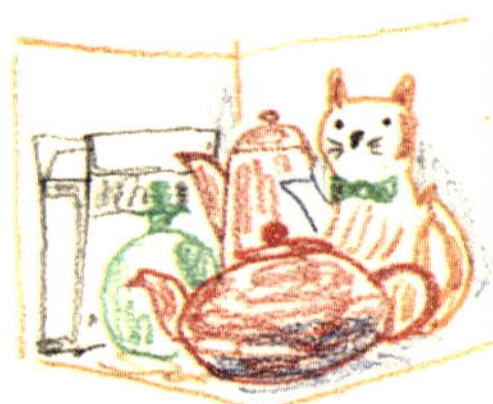
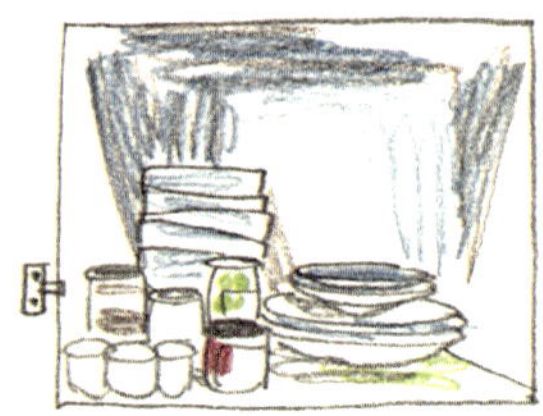
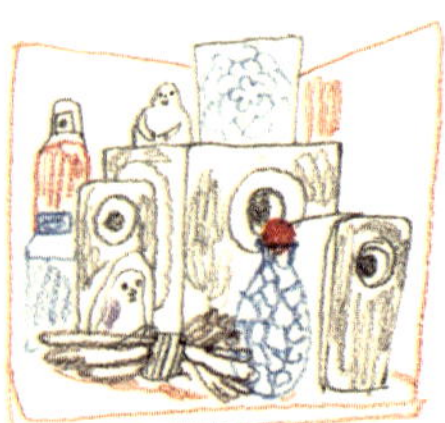
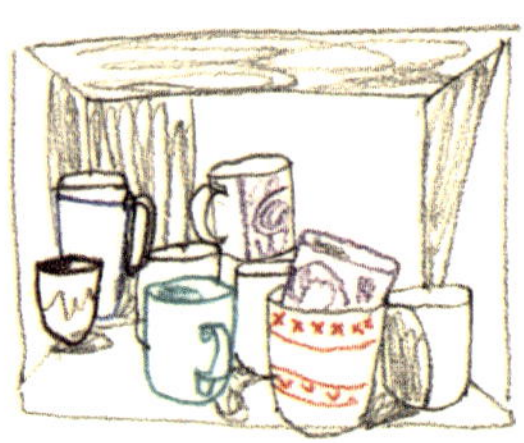
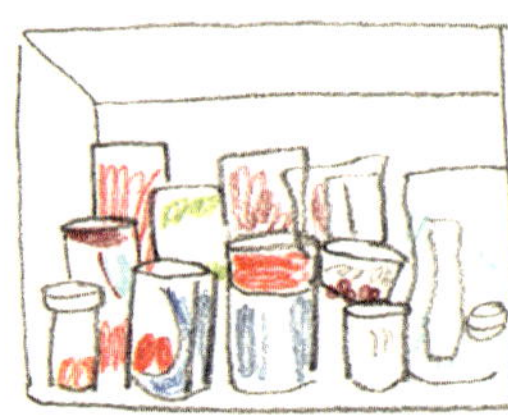

BREAKFAST

Do you make time to sit down and have a leisurely breakfast, or do you rush around getting ready to go out at the same time as eating? Do you have the same thing for breakfast every day? My old roommate used to say she could tell which direction I'd taken because she'd see my toast crusts dropped on the sidewalk near our house. What would be your ideal breakfast? Can you make it to draw? Perhaps you can go to a diner and find the perfect pastry.

You can draw a picture of your breakfast before you eat it, or when it is half-eaten or finished (an empty plate). Draw as you eat, not worrying about any crumbs that might fall on your pages, or photograph your food to draw later. If your own breakfast is not particularly inspiring, look at some food blogs for interesting ideas.

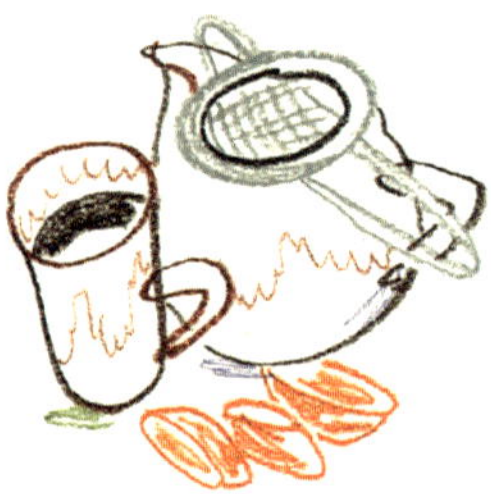
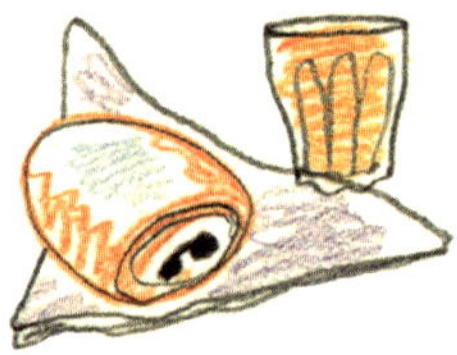
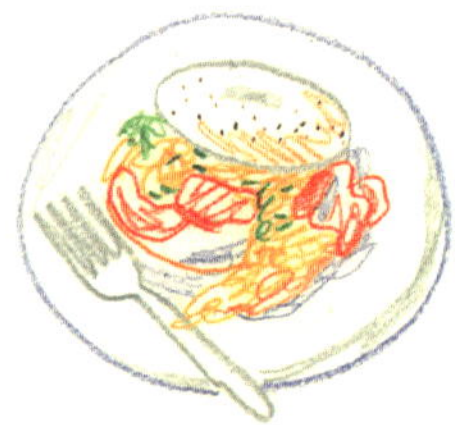
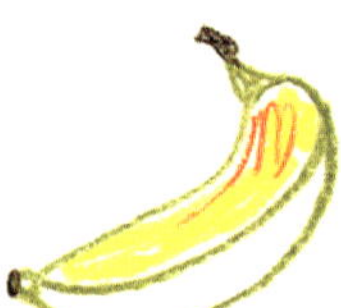
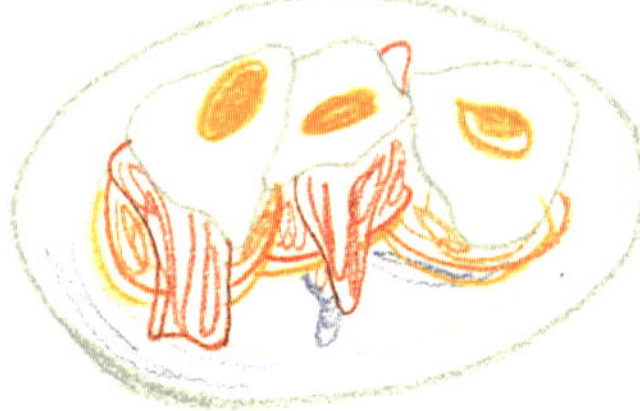
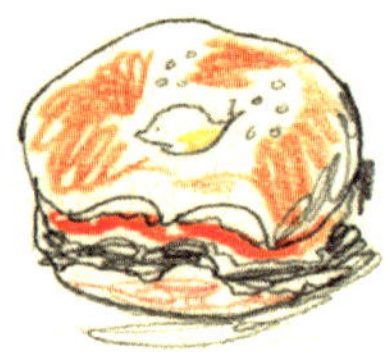

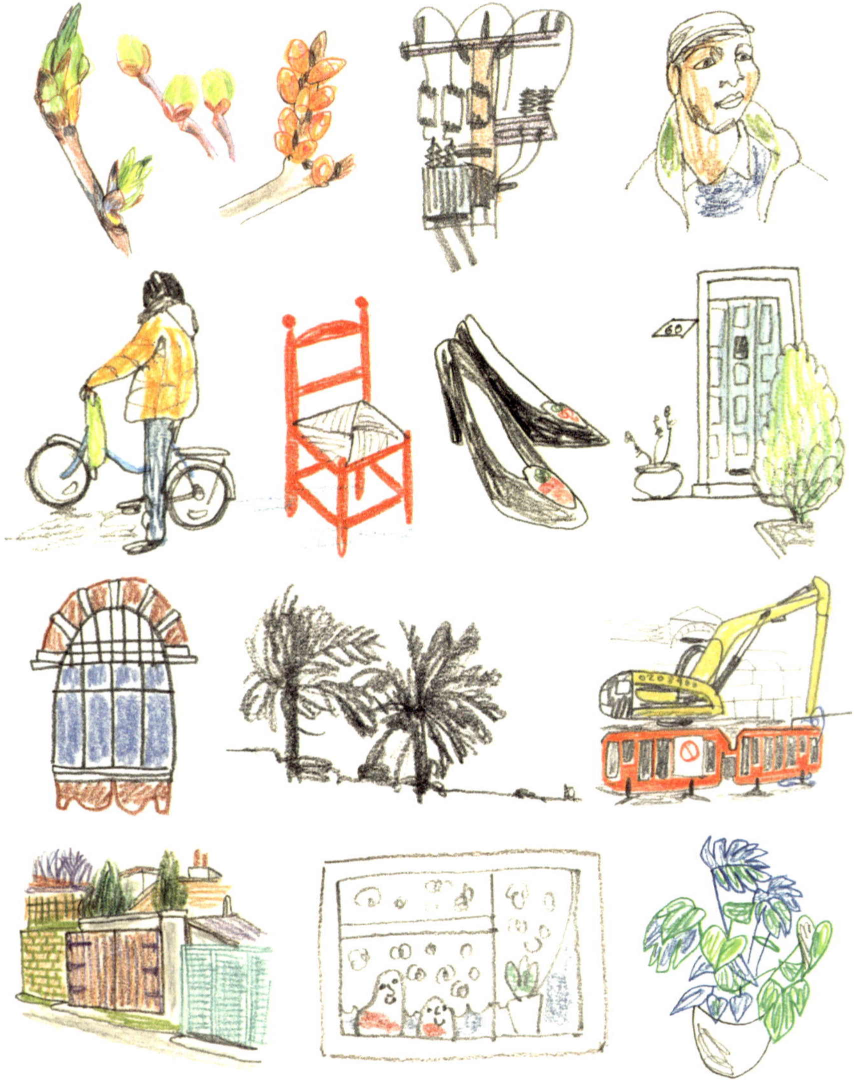
60

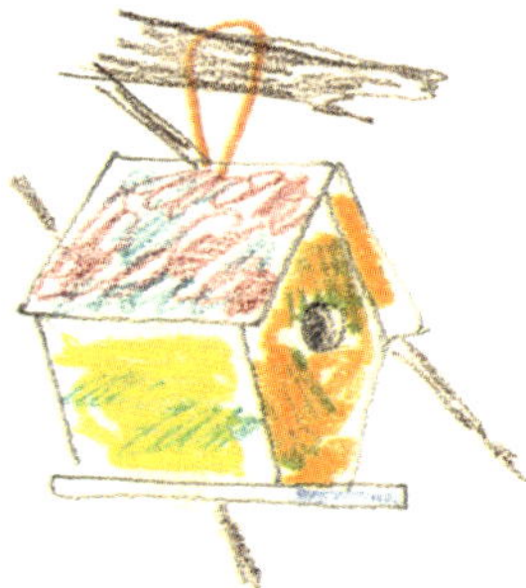

Spring

This is the season when life gets going again. Take walks around your neighborhood or go somewhere new and draw telephone poles, construction sites, skylines, or people going about their daily business. Notice what's been left outside houses after spring cleaning; you can find all kinds of interesting junk. As the season progresses, the natural world will burst into life, and you will find beautiful buds, blossoms, and early flowers coming into bloom in city parks, yards, and throughout the countryside.

BUDS

I was surprised to notice buds growing on trees throughout the winter; apparently some form at the end of a growing season and sit dormant until spring, covered in protective waxy or furry layers.

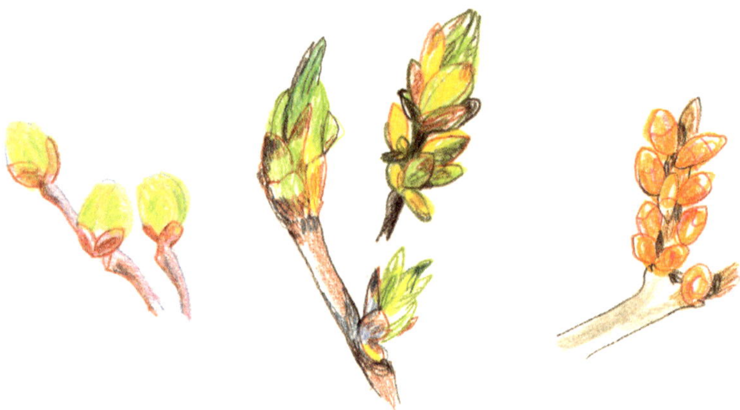

Look for buds on trees and bushes—they will appear earlier than most flower buds—on the ends of shoots or branches, nestled at junctions, on their own, or growing as part of a bigger clump. Do they give away much about what the flower or leaf will look like? Notice the color of stems and twigs; they're not always green or brown, they can be pinkish, gray, or purple.

TELEPHONE & ELECTRICITY POLES

There's something picturesque about telephone poles, the way their wires carve up the sky and landscape into geometric shapes. Look at the color of the weathered wood: green, silvery gray, or creosote brown.

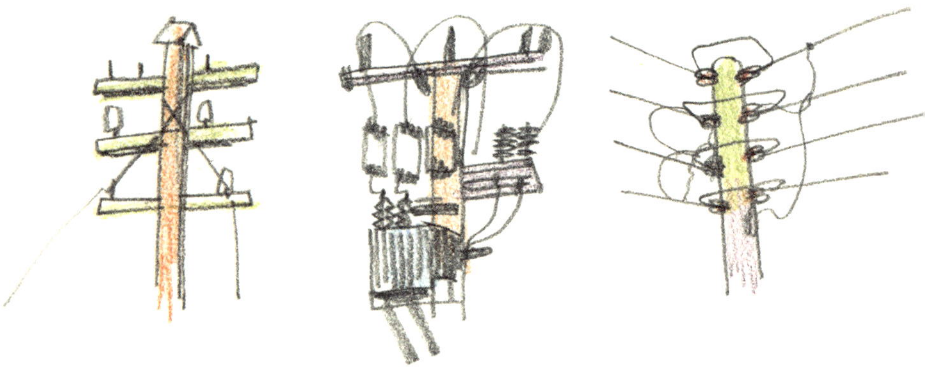

Choose two colored pencils to draw the wood of the pole. Roughly sketch it in, then add the wires with a soft graphite pencil. Sharpen your pencil and press quite hard for definition on the cables. I thought that drawing them might be a good lesson in perspective, looking at the angles at which the cables join up. But actually, my collection looks more like a plague of crane flies, cables splaying out around boxes and connectors—which is much more interesting.

PEOPLE UP CLOSE

Ask people to pose, or sketch anyone you think looks interesting. Draw people of all ages and in different situations. Look for people moving—they are difficult to sketch, but you can try to capture their character. If you want longer to draw, use online sources. Look for color on the face, and sketch that first. Make the tonal marks in the same directions as the planes of the face. Look for shadows or wrinkles.

When drawing features, use as few lines as possible. What shapes are the nose and lips? If you draw a nose using one line, will it be pointy? Wiggly? Long? Use the same approach for the head. Imagine the face as one abstract shape; try to draw it without worrying if it looks like them. Start the outline of the face somewhere near the top of the head; cover it with hair if it's not accurate. Notice where the eyes are positioned on the head; probably not right at the top unless you are looking from a low angle.

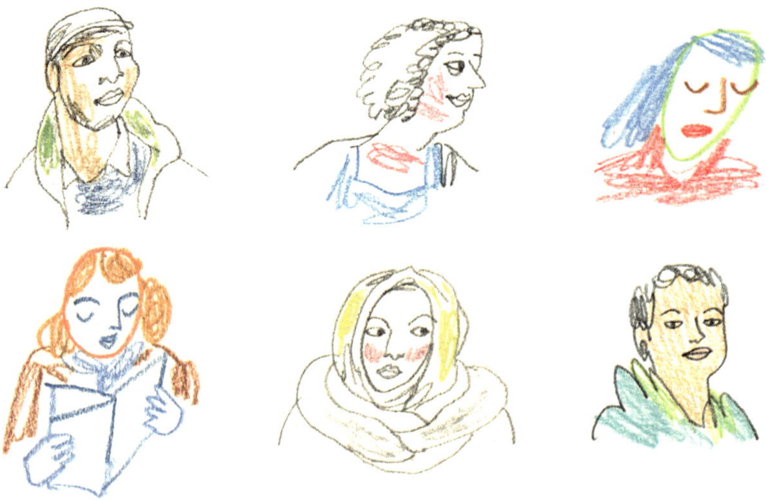

PEOPLE IN THE DISTANCE

Look for people waiting around or relaxing; hopefully, they'll be still for a while. Find them in cafés, parks, beaches, stations, art exhibitions, or markets. Are they holding anything interesting? Look for outfits that might be fun to draw, or that conceal or show off the body. Do they cast a shadow? In which direction do their feet point? Can you see their face? What mood are they in?

Try to draw quickly, before the person moves. Choose a couple of colors, perhaps one for a garment and one for their skin, and lightly sketch in those areas. Use the color patches to help you decide where to add detail, using a sharp, soft pencil. Will the lines describe the texture of a fabric or how it falls? Or the way a person moves? Try a fainter line for where sunlight hits and darker lines for shadow.

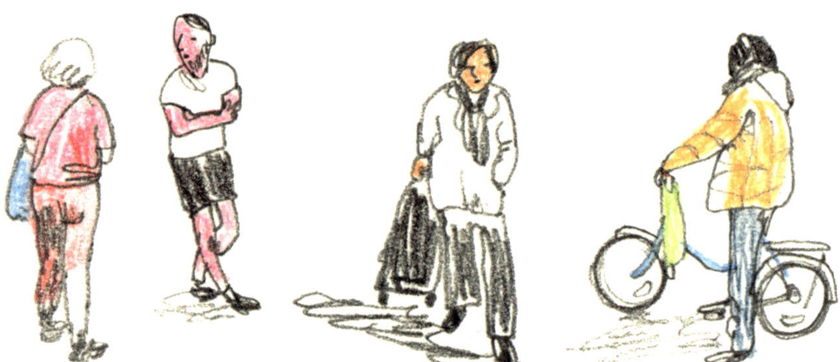

LOST OR DISCARDED THINGS

Look for junk that has been left out on the street or lost items. Single gloves draped over fences, soggy hats on fence posts, piles of cardboard, broken furniture, toys, or appliances, or garbage cans themselves. On my street, when people dump their garbage in the wrong place, other people bring more junk to the same spot and it all ends up in a mound like an accidental sculpture.

Can you see anything that looks out of place, such as colorful plastic against gray concrete or foliage, or anything arranged in an interesting way? These things probably won't be clean and tidy—your drawings can reflect that. Try drawing with loose, almost scribbly marks.

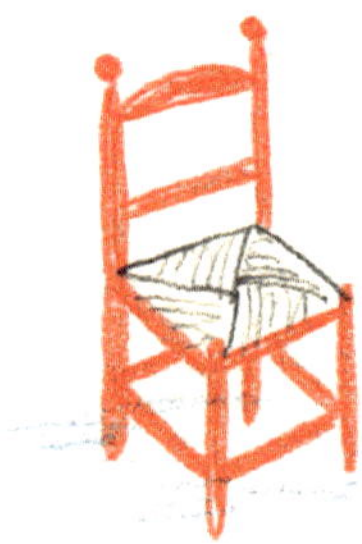
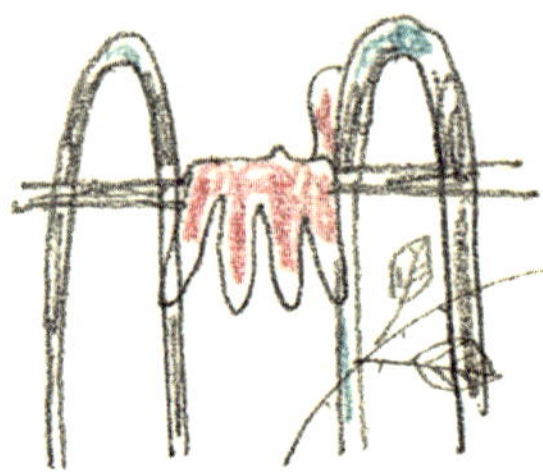
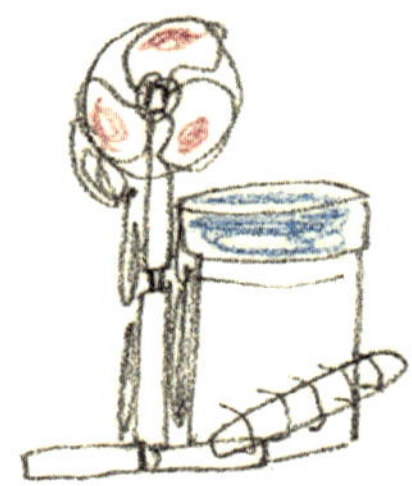
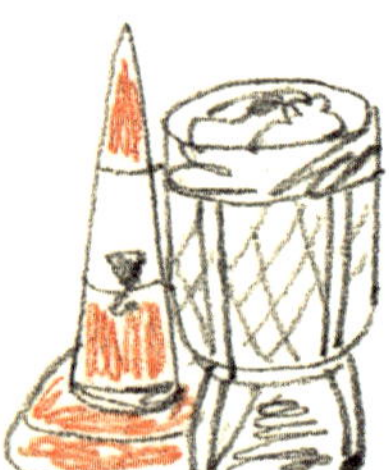
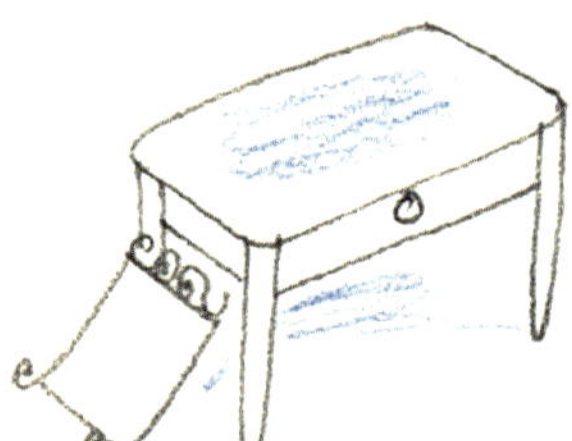
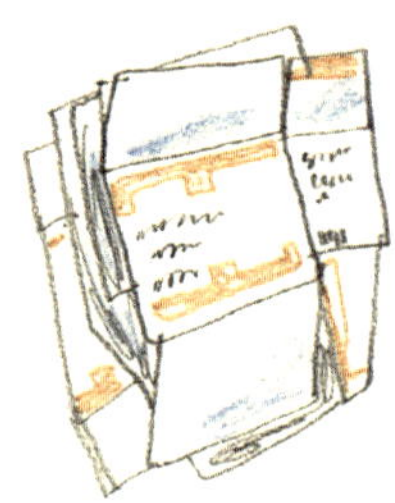

SHOES

Draw your own shoes, or those that people around you are wearing; commuters when you're on your way to work, friends or family at home. Will you draw the shoes on or off their feet? Are the feet crossed? Will you draw both shoes in a pair or just one? If shoes in real life are too ordinary, search online stores or auction sites for vintage or other styles. Or visit a shoe store or thrift shop and photograph or sketch any that you like.

Try to draw a range of shoes: sneakers, brogues, slippers, heels, work shoes, party shoes, comfortable shoes, or completely impractical shoes. Look for different textures: shiny, worn, clean, or dirty. What type of character does each shoe have? If a shoe could talk, what stories about its life would it tell?

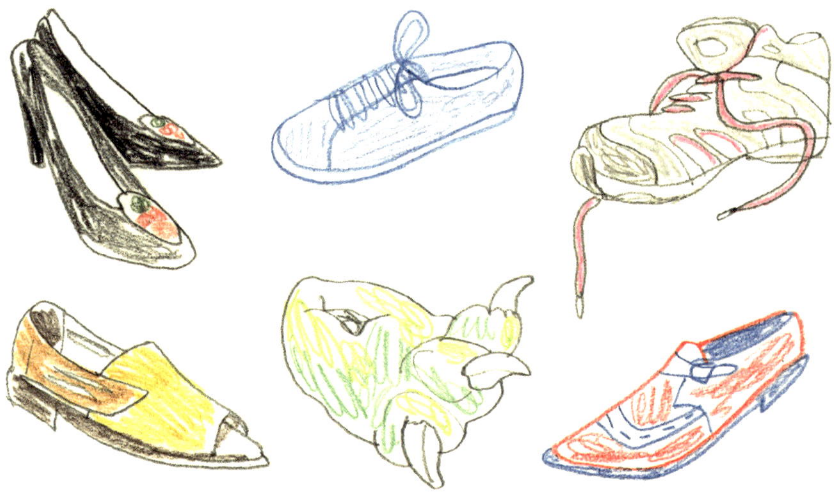

DOORS

I wanted to be able to draw without having to lurk outside houses for too long, so I drew these from photographs. Look for porches, plants, wires, garbage, style clashes with neighbors, steps, paving stones, entry systems, or ornaments. What color is the door? You can use only that color and graphite to stylize your drawing.

Many of the details you'll find on a door, such as paneling or signs, can be simplified and drawn as squares or rectangles in different sizes. If the door is set back or under a porch, there may be sharp shadows. Including these will add character and depth to your drawings.

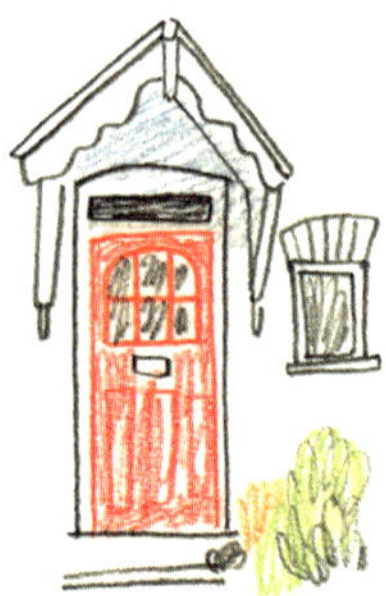
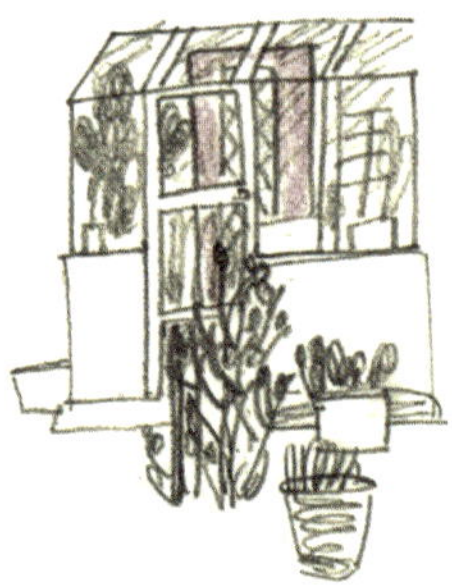

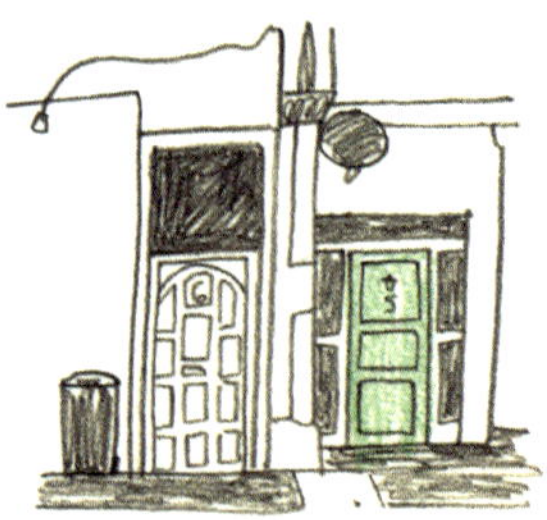
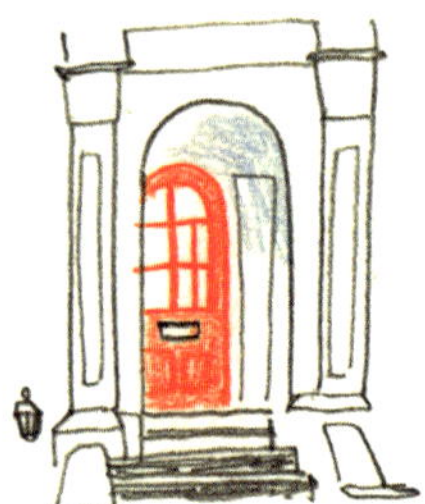
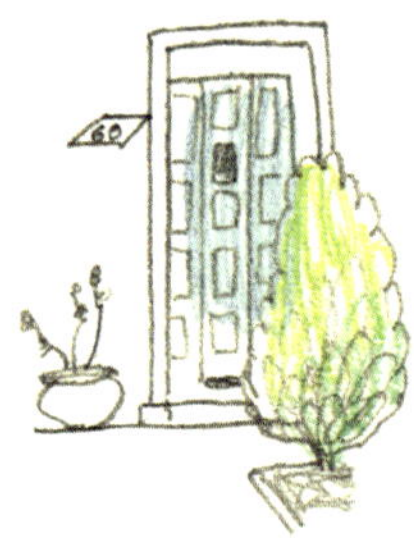

WINDOWS FROM THE OUTSIDE

What expression do different windows give to a building? Half-closed and sleepy, or narrow and shocked? Look for brightly colored curtains, shadows, brickwork, shutters, window boxes and plants, and half-closed blinds. You can draw your windows at dusk, when people haven't yet closed their curtains and you can see inside their houses.

The basic shape of a window is usually some kind of rectangle with other rectangles inside. Start by drawing all the rectangles you can see in that window. Don't worry about getting the scale or proportions exactly right. Then add any objects or ornaments that are there, or the curtains or brickwork. Does the window frame look paler than the glass, or is it a dark line?

SKYLINES

Look into the far distance to where the landscape meets the sky. You can draw rooftops, trees, streetlights, apartment or office buildings, or the shapes of hills or mountains. Try to simplify what you can see into a single line, dipping and arching to describe that edge. You can add more detail where anything stands out. Can you recognize the locations just by looking at the shapes along the line?

I used a soft, sharp pencil for these so that I could add definition where needed, and smudgier marks for overlapping textures. I loved condensing something so broad and expansive to a single, small squiggle. How many miles does your skyline cover?

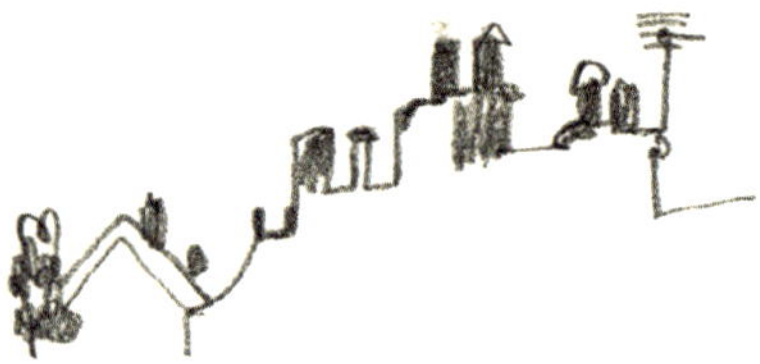

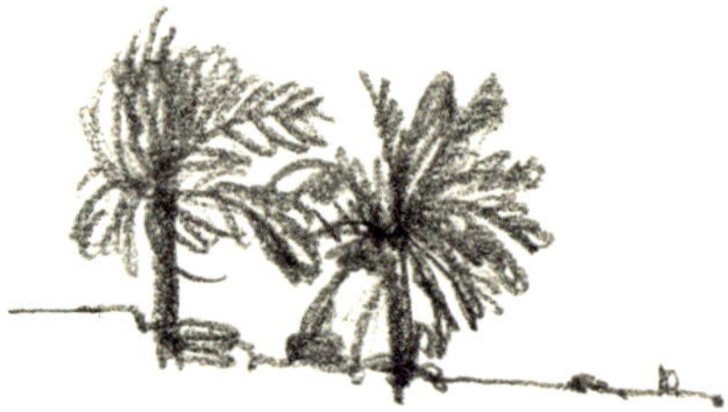

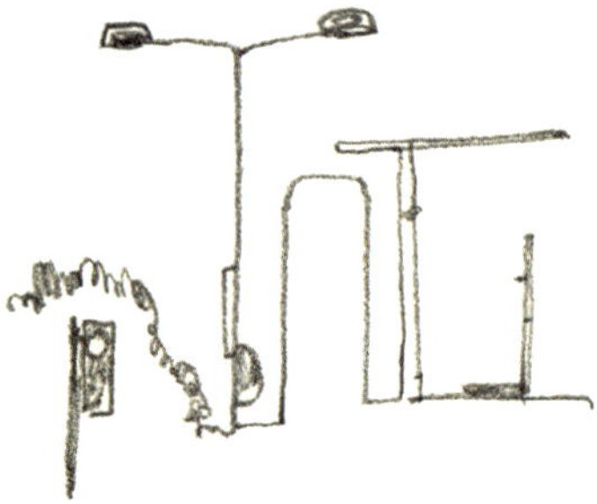

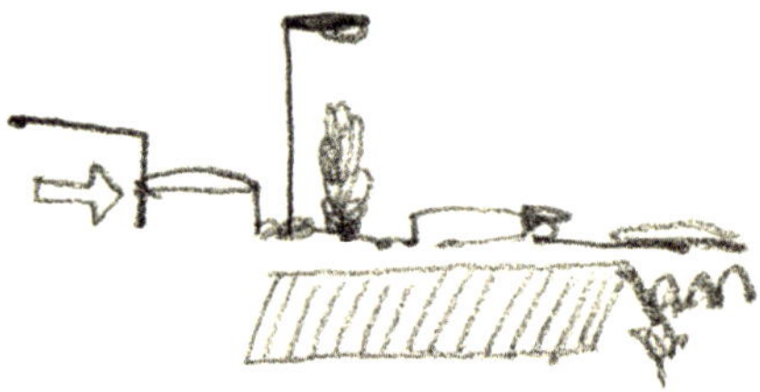

CONSTRUCTION

Look for buildings partly covered with scaffolding or held up by temporary supports; construction workers in luminous yellow jackets, standing out against gray sky or bricks; barriers and safety signs; piles of mud; cranes and heavy machinery. Excavators at rest almost look like roosting birds with their claws tucked in and necks folded over.

When drawing large scenes in a small area, think about how to abstract and simplify what you can see. You won't be able to include every window or cable; can you break the scene down into a few shapes or lines? Long, parallel lines can be difficult to draw. Try breaking them down into shorter sections and stopping the lines where they cross other lines, so you don't notice the seams in your strokes.

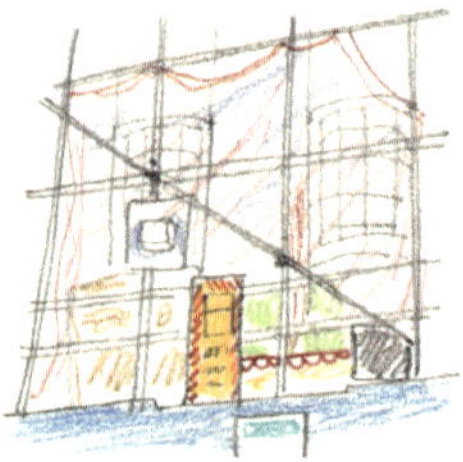

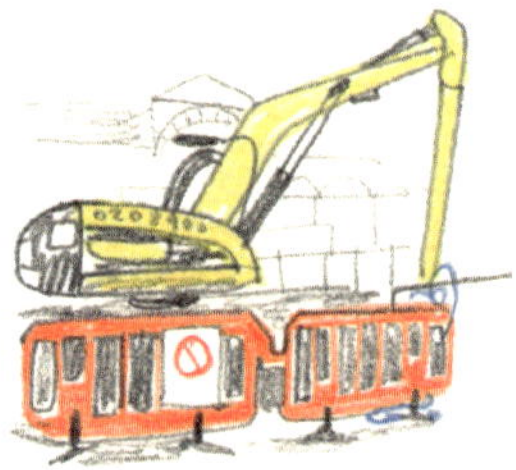

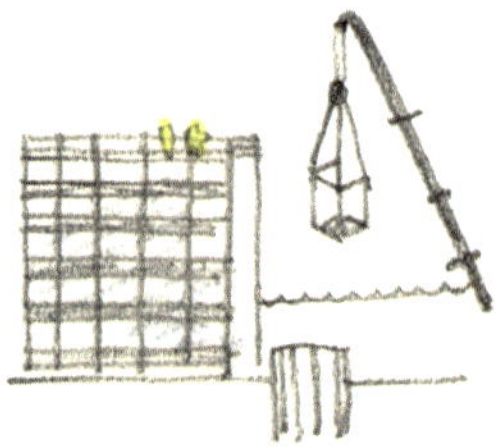

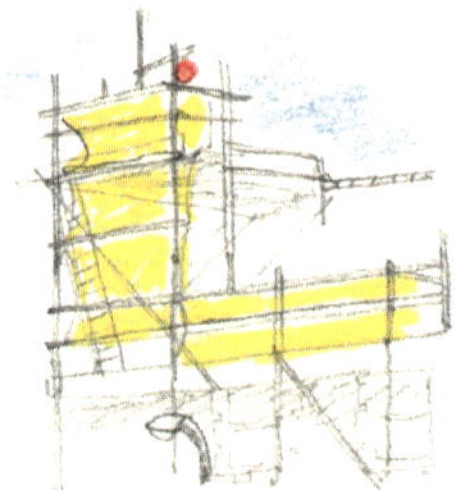

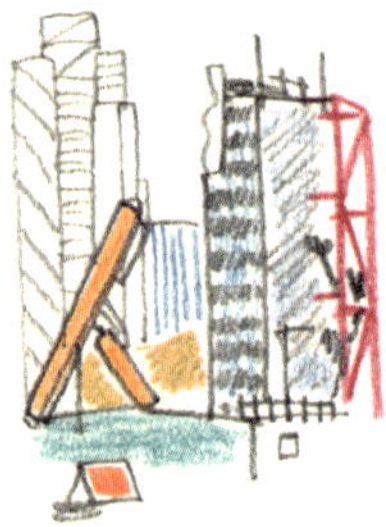

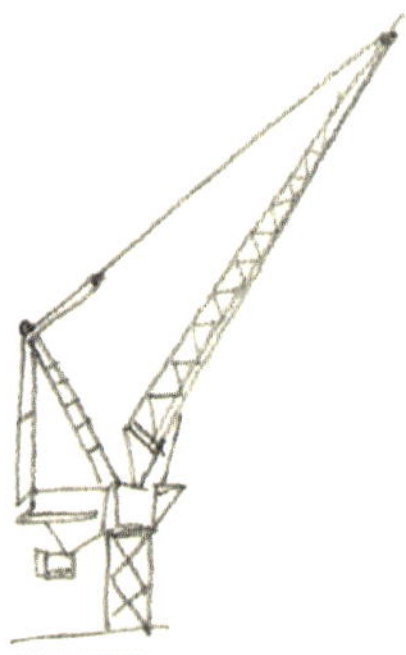

FENCES, GATES & BOUNDARY WALLS

Fences are interesting to draw because slats, pickets, bricks, planks, and posts line up against each other, making unintentional abstract patterns. Some fences are gappy and overgrown, with plants and trees bursting through, and new pieces tacked on where old pieces have fallen off. Others are freshly primed, high and fortresslike. Look for fences in different colors and styles, and notice how they connect to the fence of the neighboring property. You can imagine the yards behind them.

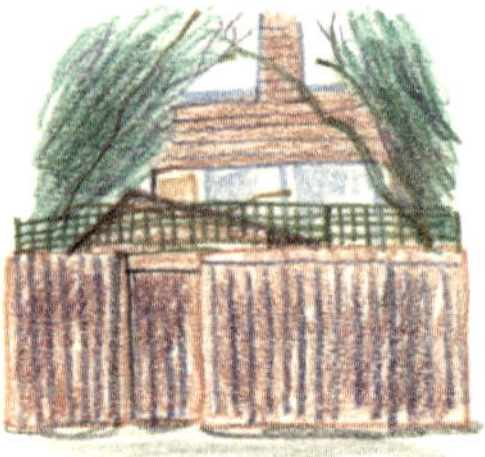

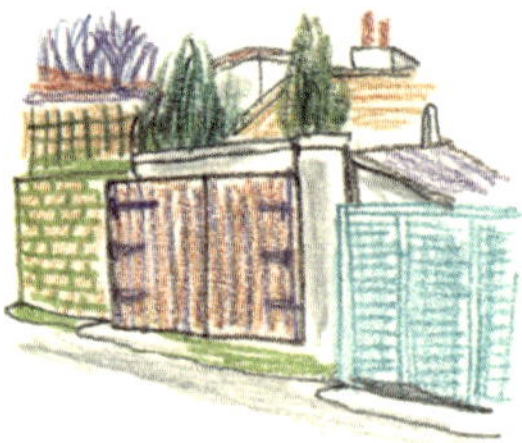

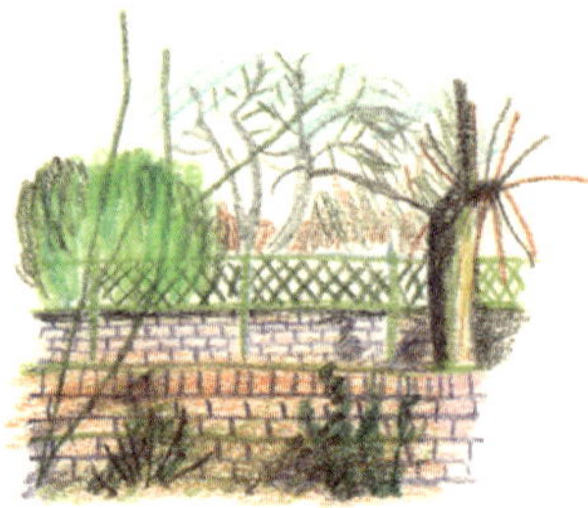

For each different section of fence, choose one base color and another color to draw the lines between the planks of wood. Look carefully; those lines aren't always black. Are there any colorful plants or trees spilling over the fence, or standing nearby and creating interesting shadows?

OBJECTS IN WINDOWS

I thought it would take a while to find enough of these to draw, but actually there were plenty of things of all shapes and sizes in people's windows—knickknacks, pets, plants, the backs of picture frames, takeout lunch in paper bags. Some items had been flattened by furniture or knocked over by curtains.

If you're drawing during the day, the room inside will probably appear to be darker than the frame. Try to draw a suggestion of any interesting shadows or reflections that you can see in the glass. A few layers of soft pencil marks on top of each other will give you this effect.

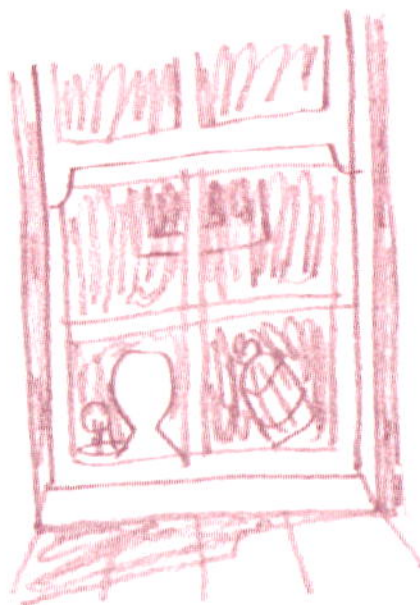
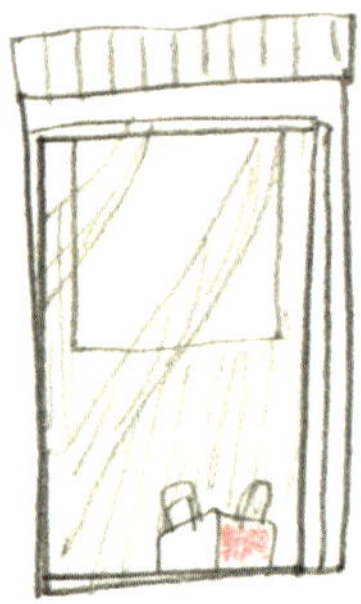
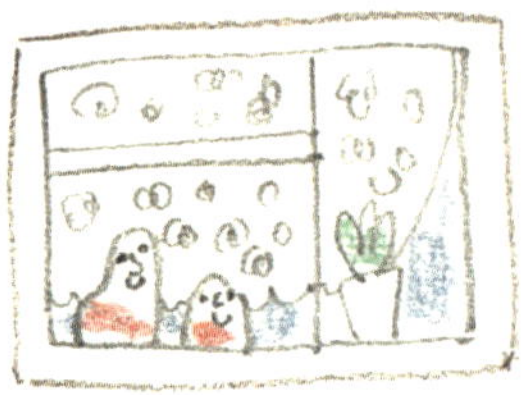
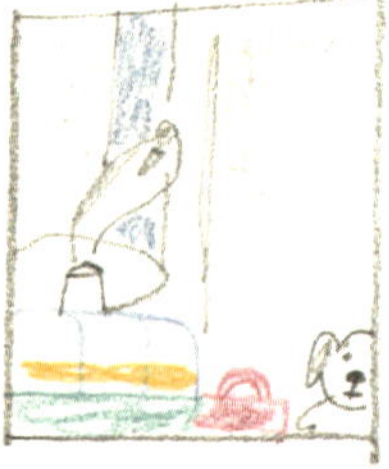
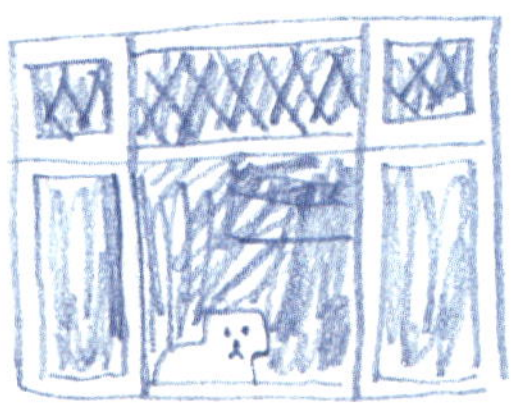
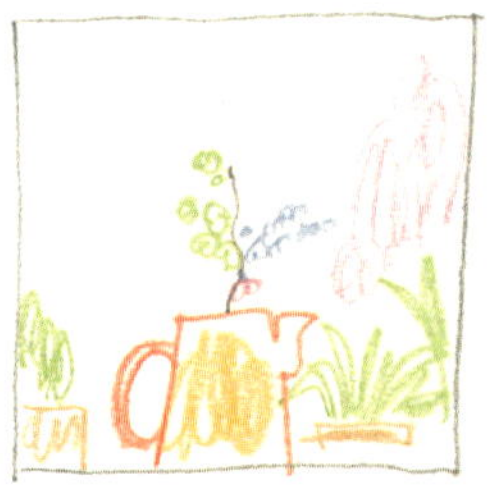

HOUSEPLANTS

If you have houseplants, are they well looked after or neglected? Well dusted and shiny or shriveled and leggy? If you don't have any, ask your friends to send you photos of theirs, go to a garden center or browse some houseplant blogs. Look for interesting containers too. You can draw close-up sections of a plant if you prefer. I love fleshy, succulent plants, flopping over the side of their containers like they're trying to get somewhere.

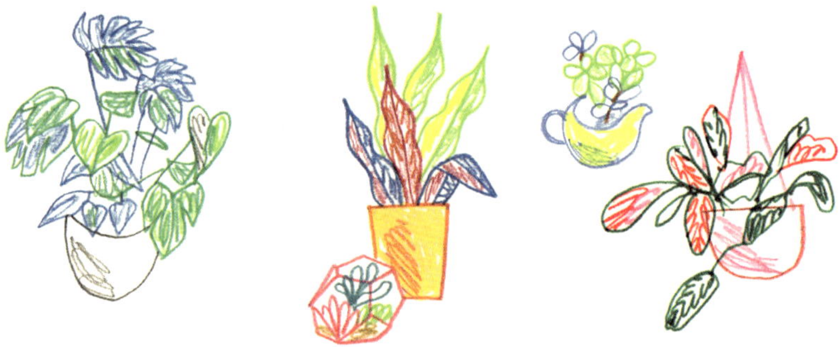

I drew these with colored pencils and markers. Keep colored pencils sharp so you can make defined lines as well as softer patches of color, or use different thicknesses of marker. Try using thicker lines for the side of a leaf that's in shadow, and finer lines for the patches where light reflects. You don't have to use the actual colors of your houseplants.

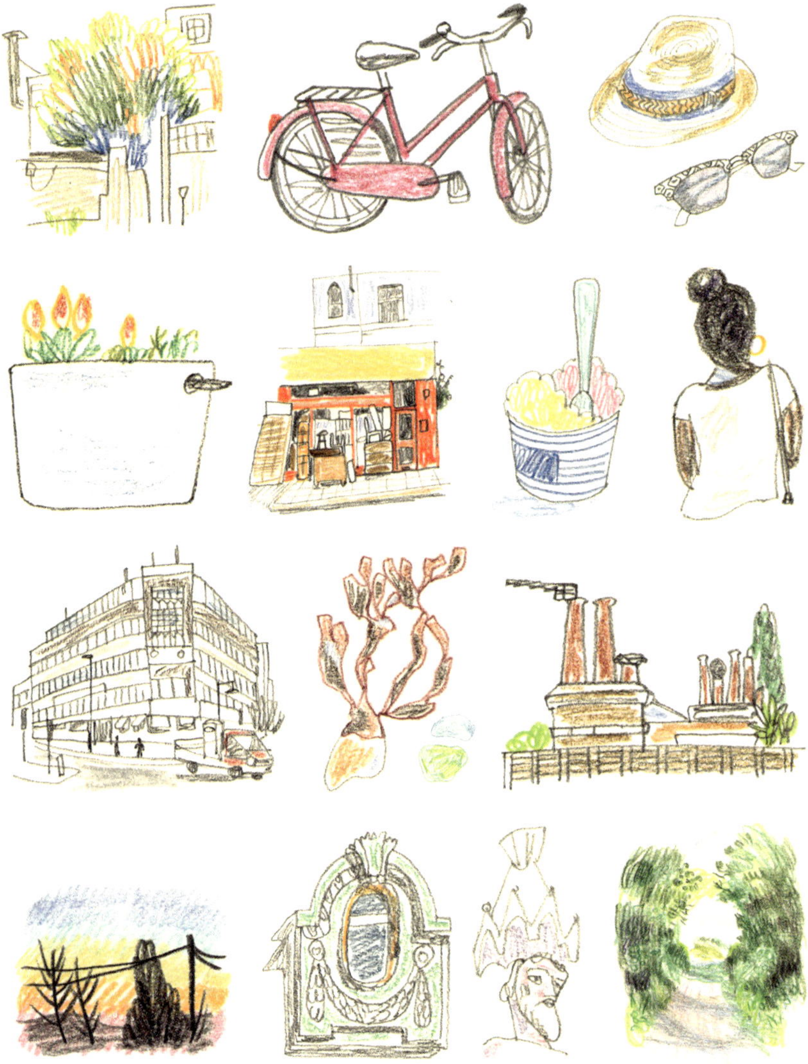

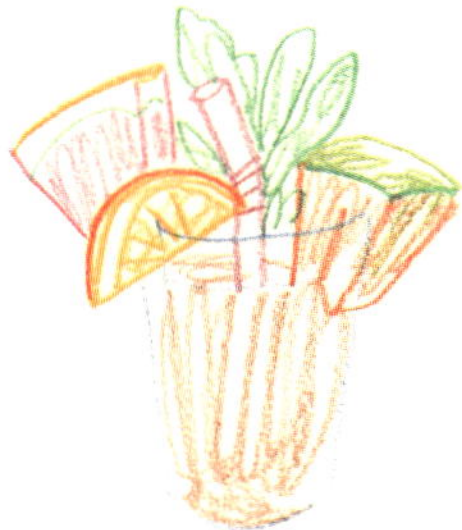

Summer

Make the most of an abundance of light and color! Let the sunshine tempt you to draw outside and look for shimmering trees, melting ice creams, favorite warm-weather clothes freshly uncovered from under piles of sweaters, and sunsets on long, warm evenings. Make yourself a tall, cool drink, decorate it with fruit, and see how you can best capture the bright colors. If you find yourself on the beach, see what you can collect there that might be interesting to draw.

TREES WITH LEAVES

Before you start, look at where the light hits the tree. What color is that patch? It might not be green. Then look at the parts of the tree that are in shadow, almost blue or cool purple. Look for round, cloud-topped trees, or wandlike trees with smaller puffs of leaves, or trees growing in odd places, or with brightly colored leaves.

Choose two or three pencils to work with in a selection of the colors in the tree. Loosely sketch the lightest area—press quite hard—then add the shady patches in the same way, pressing a little less hard. Using a sharp pencil, add finer marks to suggest twigs, branches, or leafy texture, and any other interesting details, but don't worry about drawing every leaf.

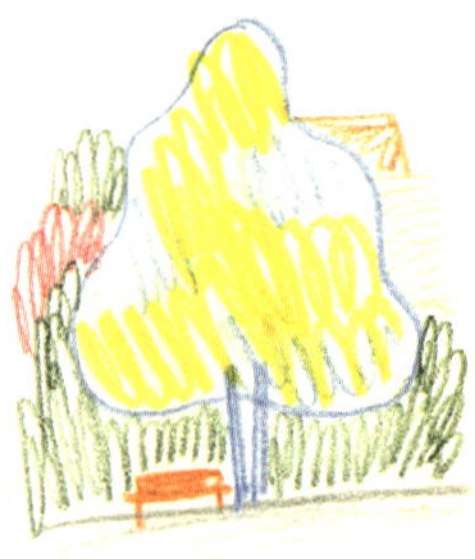
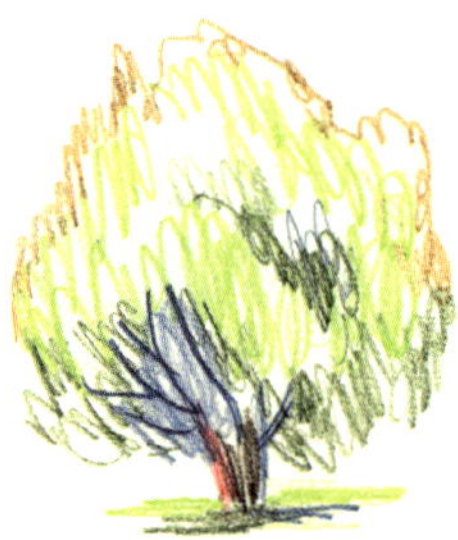
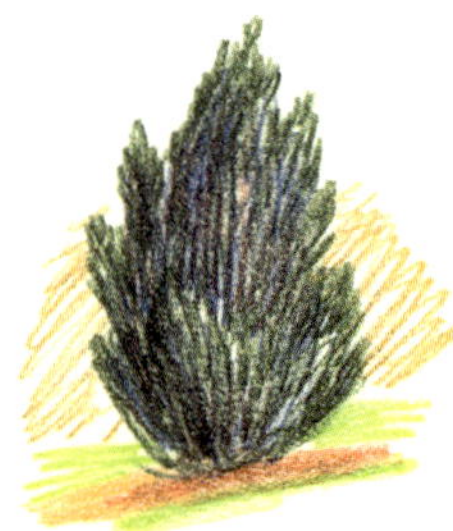
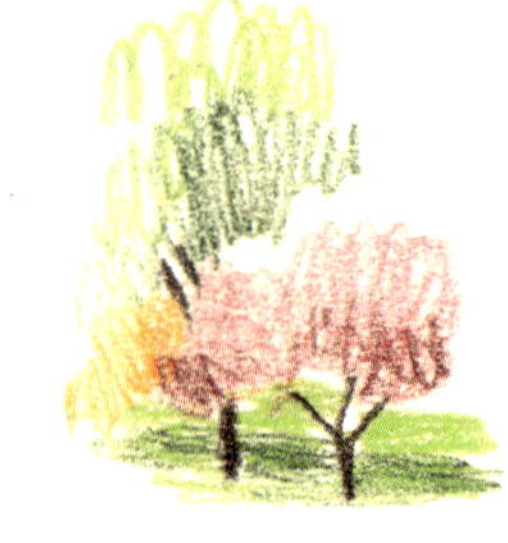
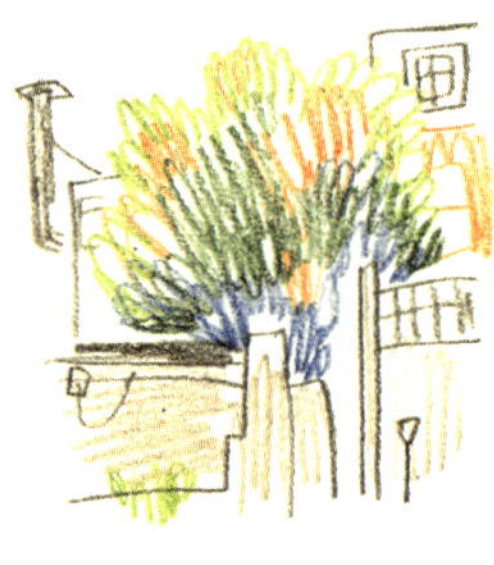
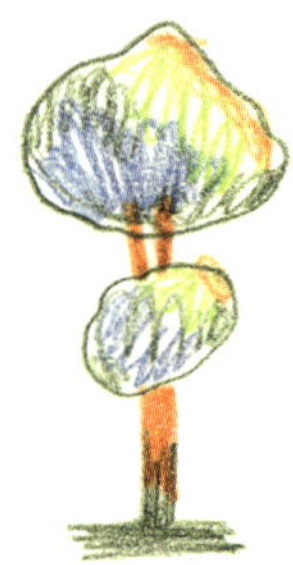

BICYCLES

Bikes are really hard to draw. Circles are difficult, and if you don't get the dimensions of the bike frame quite right, the whole thing will look a bit weird. But that's OK; don't worry if your drawings look wobbly or out of proportion. You could even make it a feature, and celebrate the weirdest one.

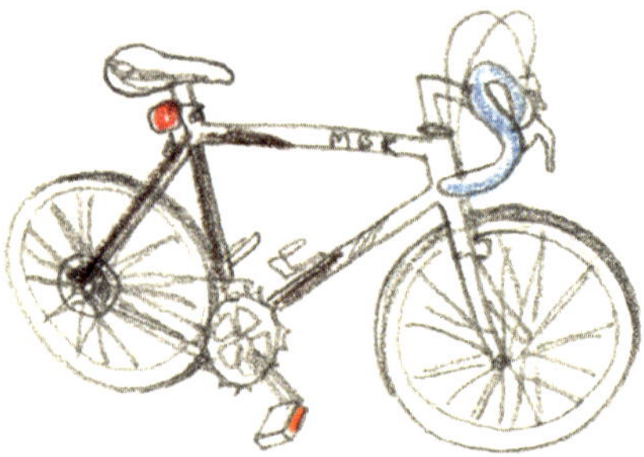

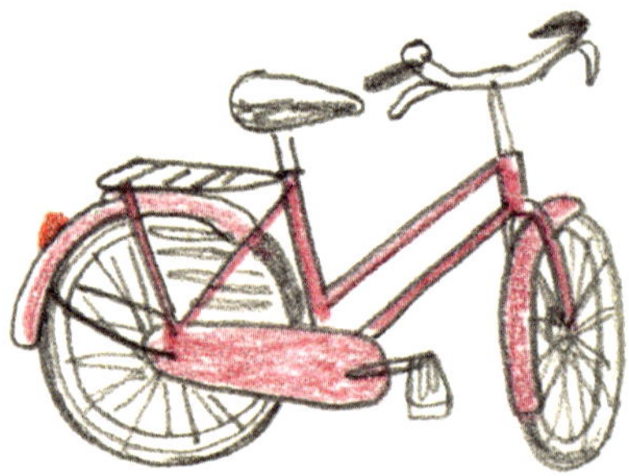

Unless you are looking from a low-down, side-on viewpoint, the wheels probably won't look perfectly circular. Look at the frame first and imagine it on its own—what shape does it make? Look for different types of handlebars, baskets, panniers, or other accessories. You can draw several bikes locked together, although this would be even more complicated.

SUMMER CLOTHES & ACCESSORIES

Find your favorite summer clothes and draw them, lying flat or on hangers, or take photos of clothes in stores to draw from later. If anyone you know wears nice outfits in the summer, you can draw their clothes instead.

Choose anything bright that catches your eye, and don't worry about getting any patterns completely accurate. This is a good opportunity to use bold colors. You can create marks that are loose and wiggly to give the impression of folds and creases.

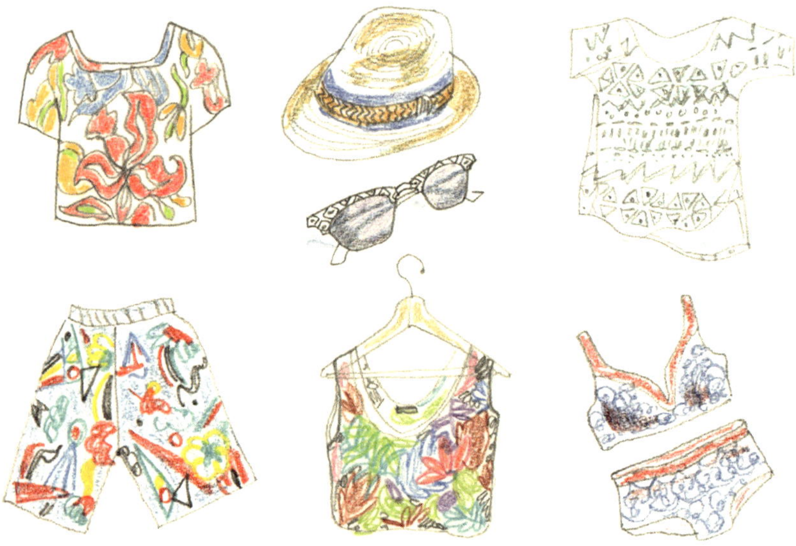

GARDEN DECORATION

Have a look in parks or yards for any interesting decorations such as bird feeders, nest boxes, novelty plant containers, statues, and plastic animals. Are they clean and new or weathered and covered with moss? Are the plant containers well kept, brimming with colorful flowers, or neglected with nothing to show but a few straggly weeds?

I like that combination of brightly colored plastic and earthy natural tones—it creates an interesting contrast. You can simplify this composition by drawing a piece of garden decoration on its own, or make it more detailed and colorful by including the surrounding foliage or flowers.

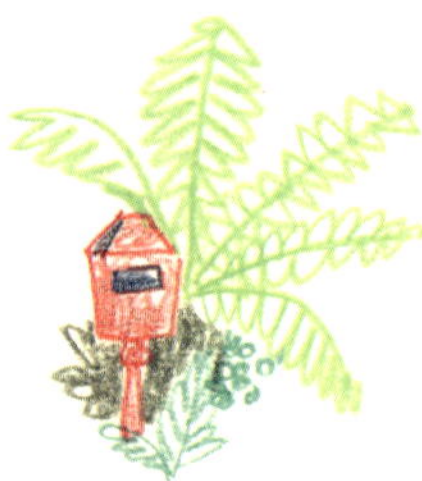

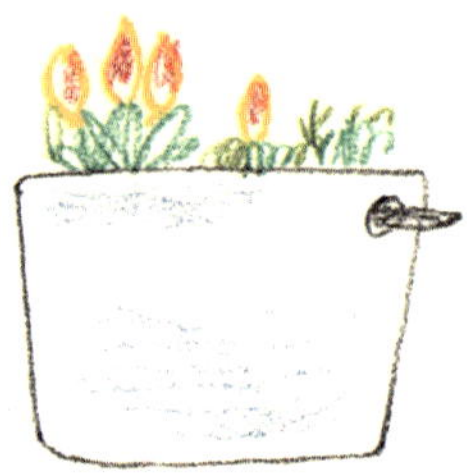

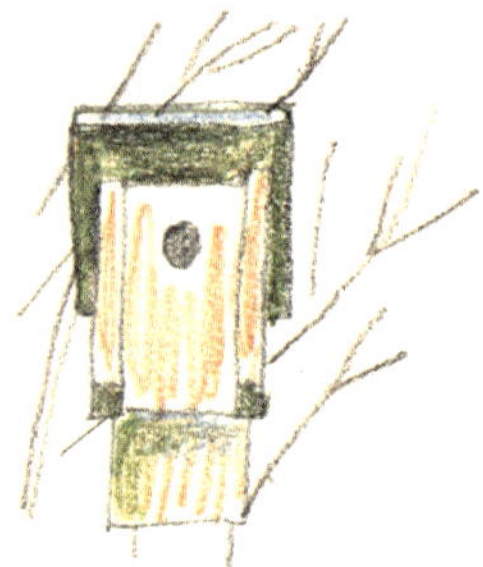

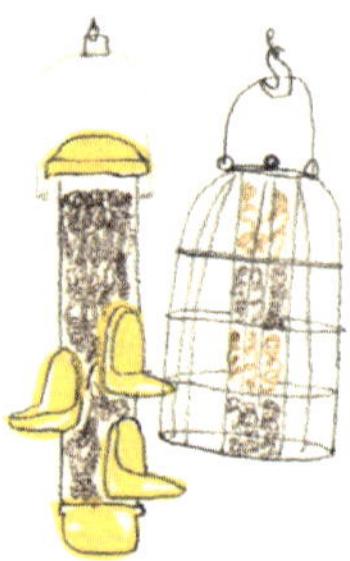

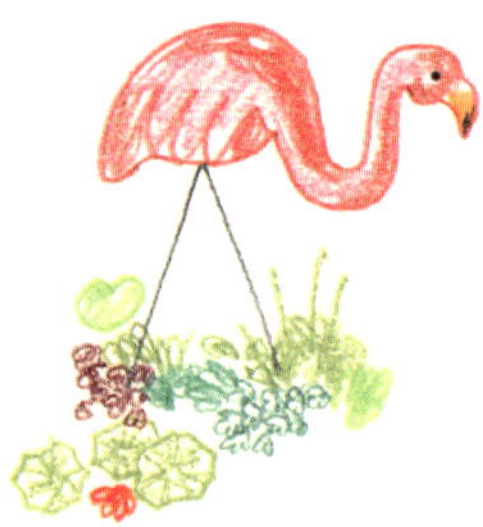

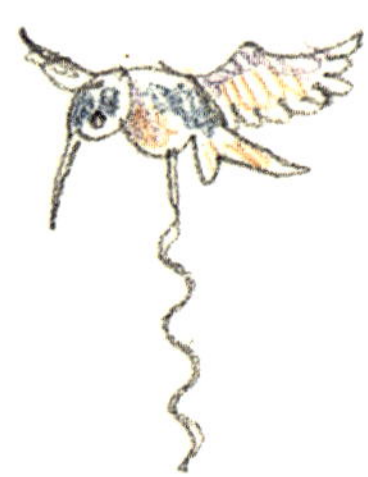

STOREFRONTS

Look for old, shabby stores, bargain stores, or thrift shops with products piled up to have as much displayed as possible. Look for out-of-date posters, sale signs, advertisements, and slogans. Upscale stores also might be fun to draw as a contrast, with luxury items and carefully curated displays. Homogenous chain stores might seem predictable and therefore less interesting to draw, but what might a drawing of one of them tell us about ourselves in a few years' time when prevailing trends have changed?

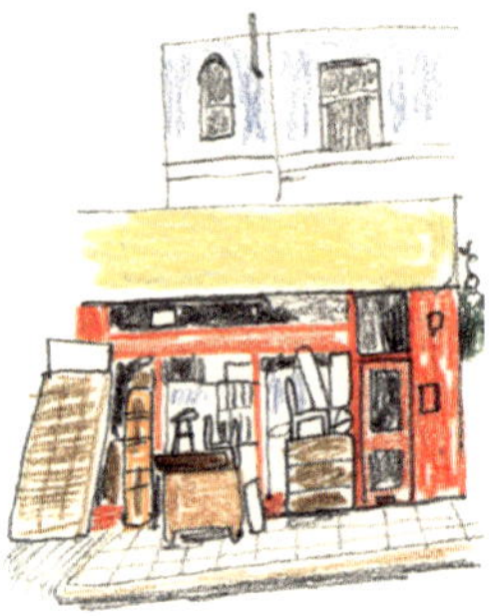

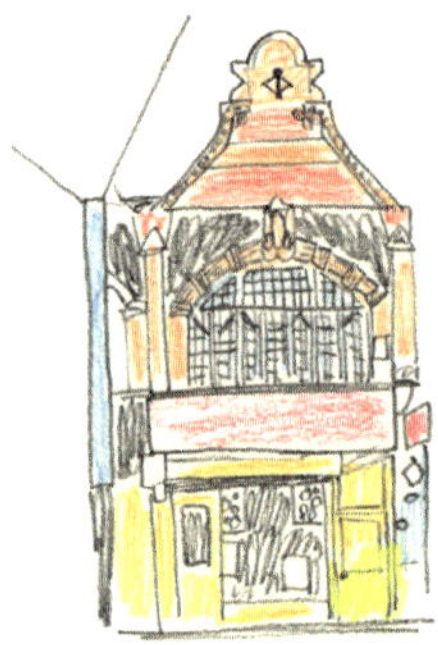

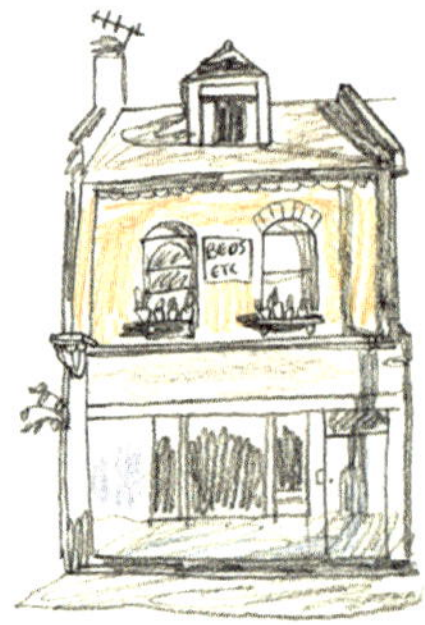

To simplify and draw the storefronts, imagine that all the details you can see are part of an abstract pattern. Include a wider area from the front of the building if you want to, or what's on the street in front of the store—this can be items for sale or just the sidewalk.

COOL TREATS

Buy yourself some summery treats and draw them quickly before they melt. Choose something that will be fun to draw, with cocktail umbrellas, slices of fruit, dribbles of sauce, layers of ice cream, straws, or a decorative glass. If you can't hold your treat with one hand and draw with the other, ask someone else to hold it for you.

It might be fun to make "before" and "after" drawings, perhaps a tall sundae glass filled with different colored ice cream and fruit, then eat the contents and draw the empty glass with just a few smears around the edges.

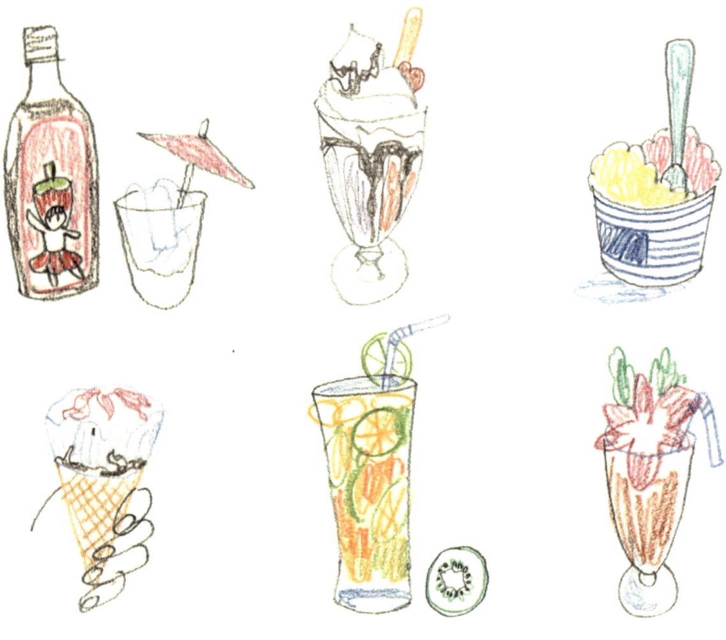

BACKS

Whenever you're waiting in a line or just passing the time, you have an ideal opportunity to draw people's backs. How does each person stand? Hunched over, leaning, or upright? Are they carrying anything, a shoulder bag perhaps? Try drawing some people who are moving and some who are still.

Use the direction of your marks to show the direction that the fabric of their clothes falls in. What shape does their head or hair make? Are there any interesting details on their clothes? If they are walking or running, try to capture the position of their arms to reflect this movement.

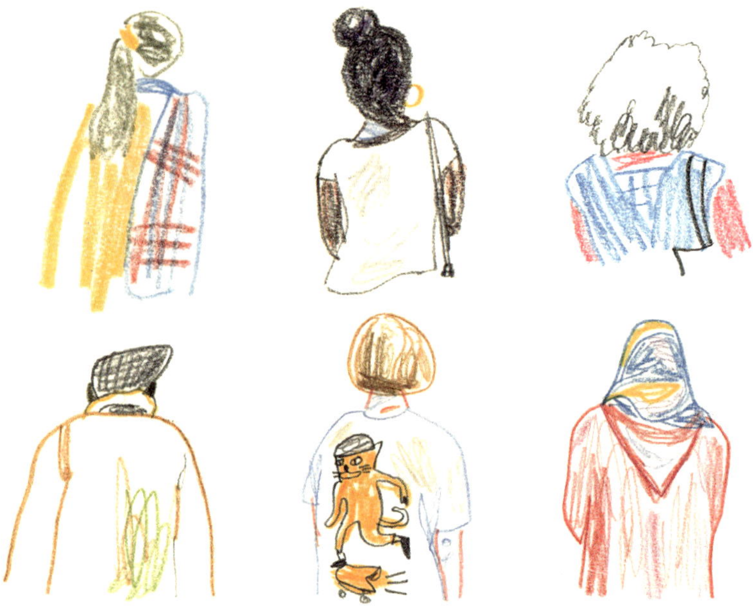

STREET CORNERS

Look for street corners or junctions that have interesting trees, buildings, or signposts. Notice how the perspective changes as you move around a corner. Compare all the angles made by roofs or roads before you make your first mark. Are there any parallel lines? Do other lines converge? If so, how sharply?

You can go somewhere new or draw corners that have some significance in your own life, such as junctions near your home, on familiar routes, or in places you like. You can simplify the drawing by choosing what you want to include and leaving out objects or people in the foreground or the detail of the buildings.

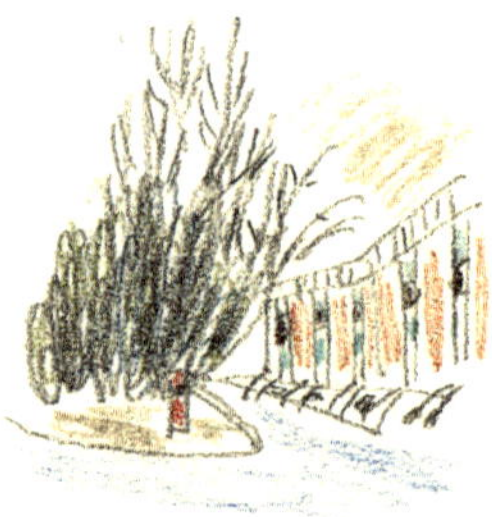
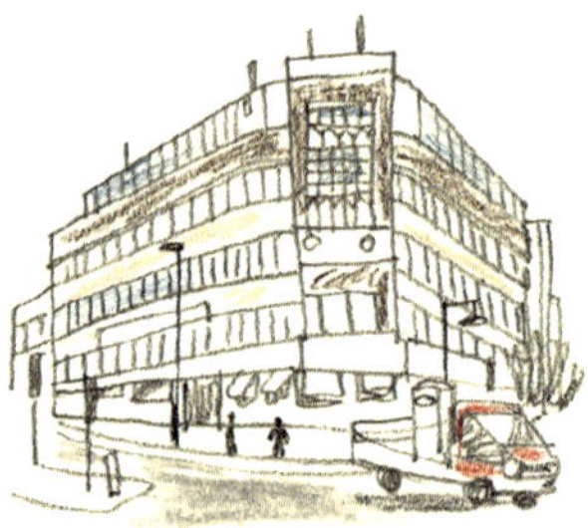
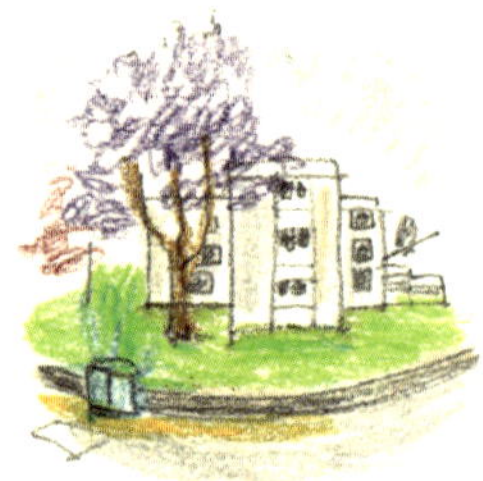
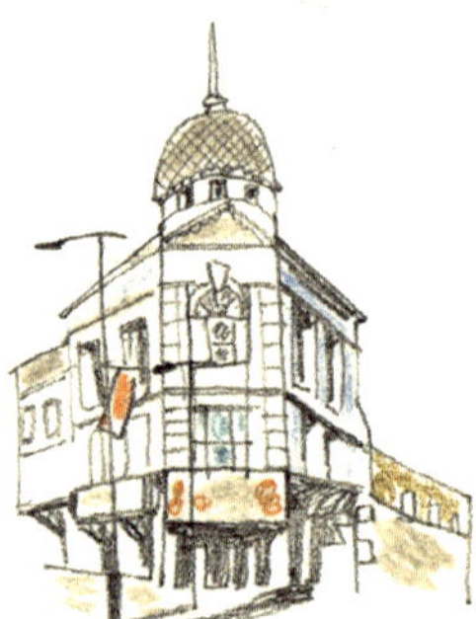
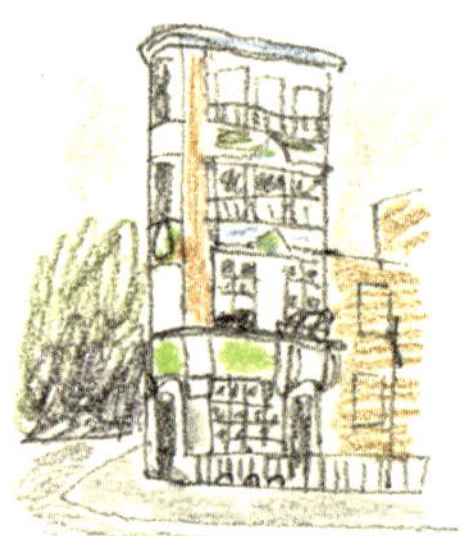
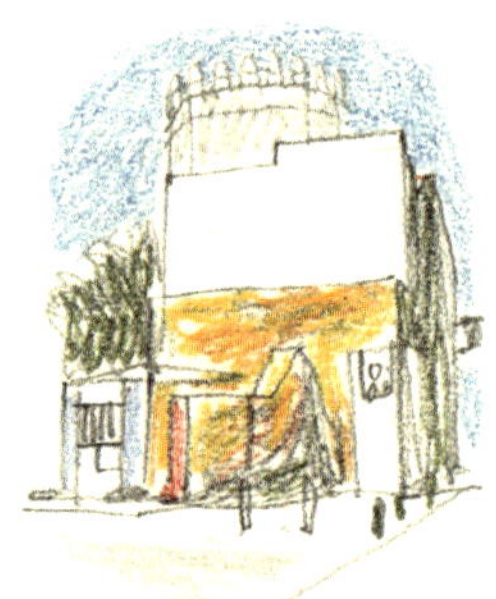

THINGS WASHED UP ON A BEACH

If you find yourself by the water, look for beautiful stones, sea glass, animal bones, seaweed, driftwood, and anything else that you find washed up there, natural or manufactured. If you can't get to the beach, look for any natural forms that catch your eye—knots in wood, pebbles, pinecones, or other odds and ends that have interesting characteristics.

Think about the journeys all the things you find have made. Where might they have come from? What did they look like originally, and how has the water changed them? Think about what might have caused the object to develop its shape or color.

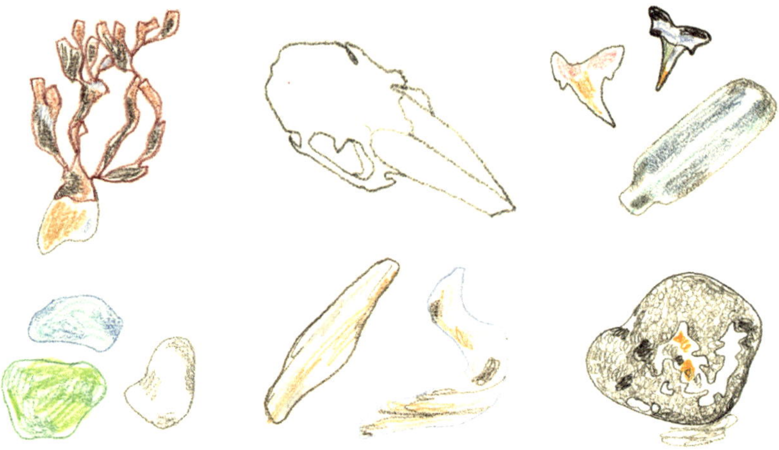

ROOFTOPS

There are various things commonly found on our rooftops that reflect the human activity within. Chimneys from when we relied on working fireplaces and TV aerials and satellite dishes added much later, many now no longer in use. Old and new apparatus wired together in robotlike shapes, dancing mischievously along the skyline.

There is so much variety in chimneys. My instinct is to anthropomorphize them, and see them as stubby, gesturing hands. If the sky is bright, your drawings can be silhouettes, or add more detail and color if you can see it. You can draw only the chimneys, or you can add in the other features found beside them on rooftops.

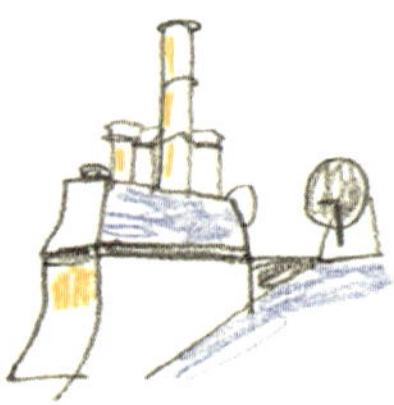
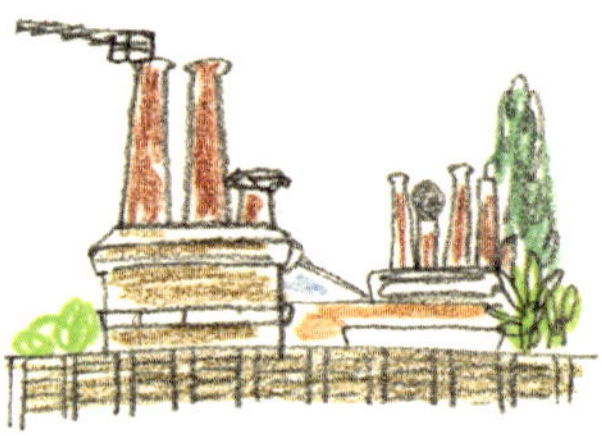
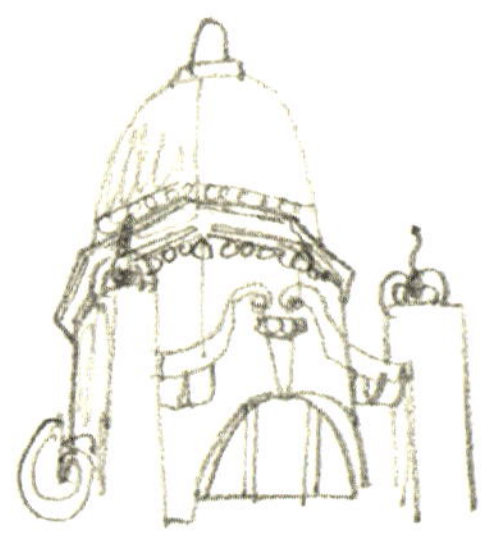
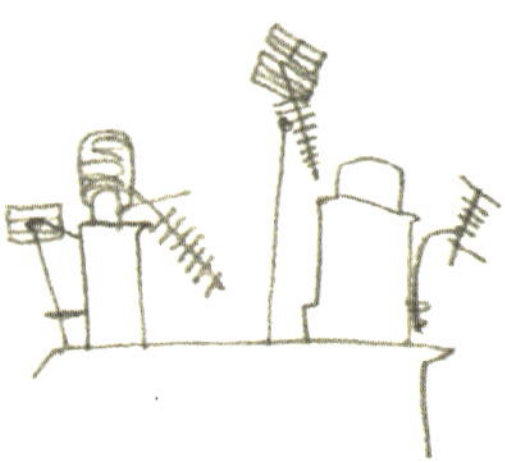
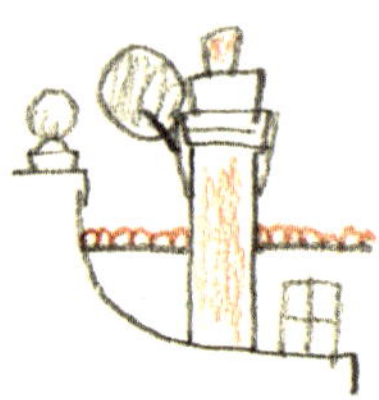
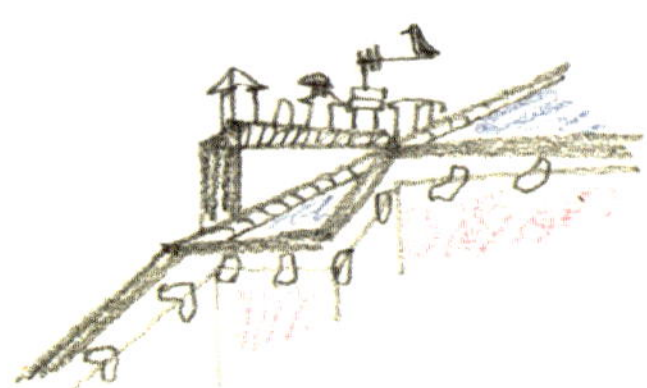

SUNSETS

Draw from real life if possible—skies change quickly, and it's satisfying to capture them. Or use photographs; I had a lot of pictures of sunsets, and it was fun to look at them again. Try different locations, or use the same one if there's a view you like. Look for clear skies; perfect gradients; delicate, dramatic, or heavy clouds; and interesting silhouettes on the skyline.

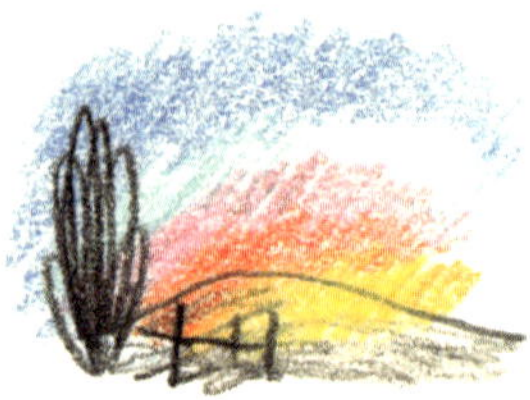

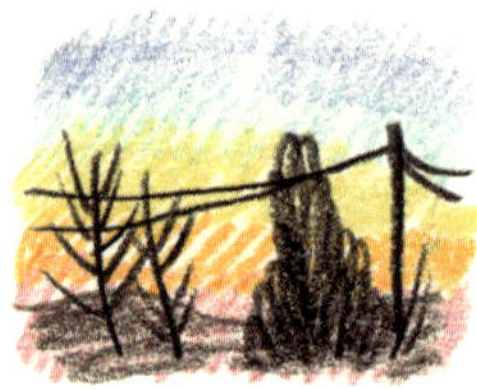

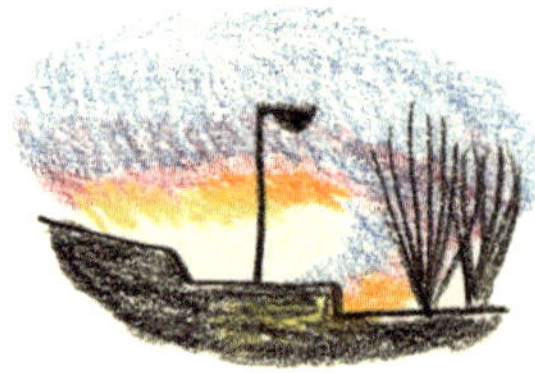

Before drawing the foreground, start drawing the lightest part of the sky with a colored pencil. If it's very pale, you could leave that part of the paper empty. Notice how the colors fade to pink, blue, purple, or gray; add these colors next. Experiment with marks; color lightly, adding delicate layers for an even tone or coarser marks to look like clouds. Is the foreground black, or are there layers of purple or gray within it?

ARCHITECTURAL DETAILS

This can be an interesting detail in the structure of a building or something more unusual that's been added. You can draw interesting doors, windows, or porches, religious iconography, neoclassical figures, post-modern designs, or any architectural detail on a building or that people have chosen to attach to their homes. You might notice clashes of style, where newer modifications have been added alongside older designs.

Will you draw the whole of the feature or focus on only part of it? If you were to simplify and draw the whole feature as one shape, what would it look like? Try drawing a basic shape, then add some contours or shadows in a different color.

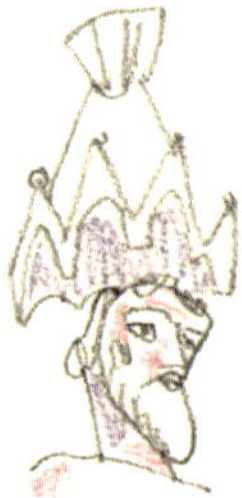
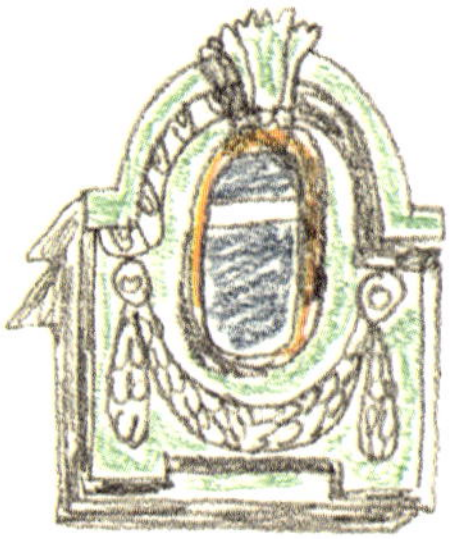
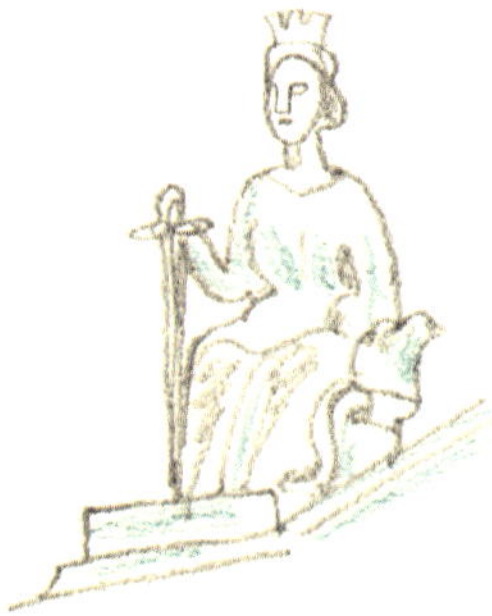
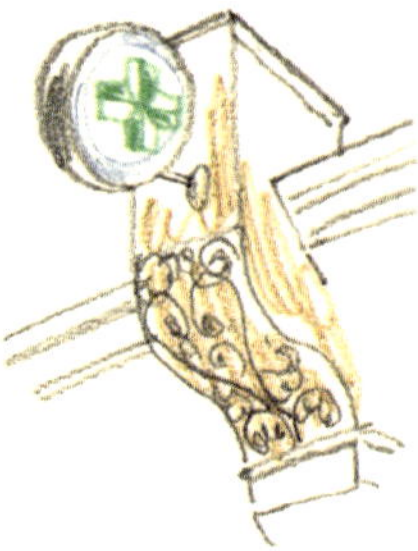
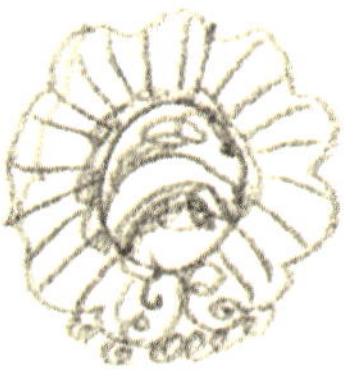
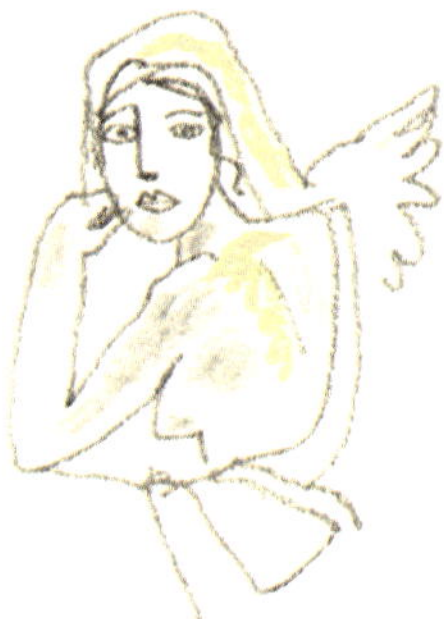

VIEWS DOWN A STREET OR TRAIL

This is a good exercise in perspective. Find an interesting street or pathway in any landscape, urban or rural. Country trails can look like tunnels when trees touch overhead. Look for color in the light and shade. How does the weather affect the light? Where do shadows fall? Are they soft or sharp? How do different elements in the scene overlap? Can you simplify by including detail in the foreground but omit them in the distant view? Do colors in the foreground vary from the background?

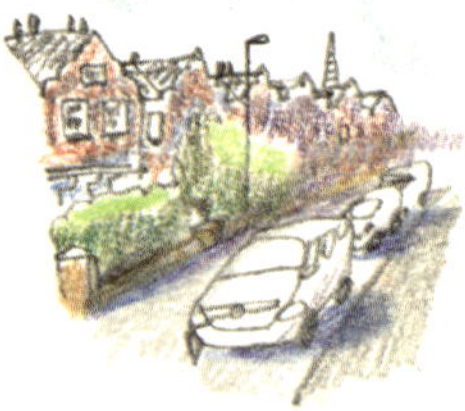

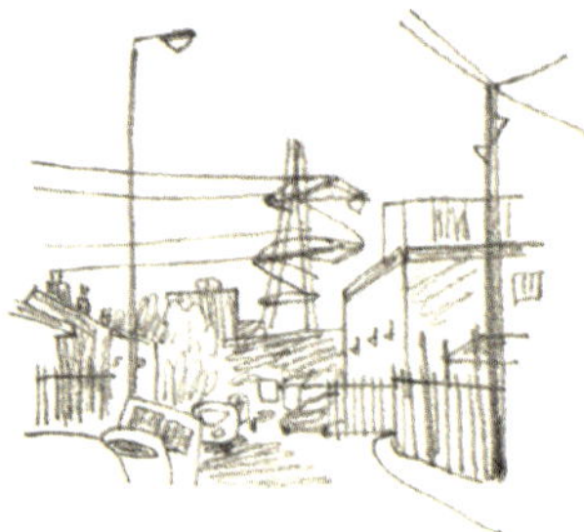

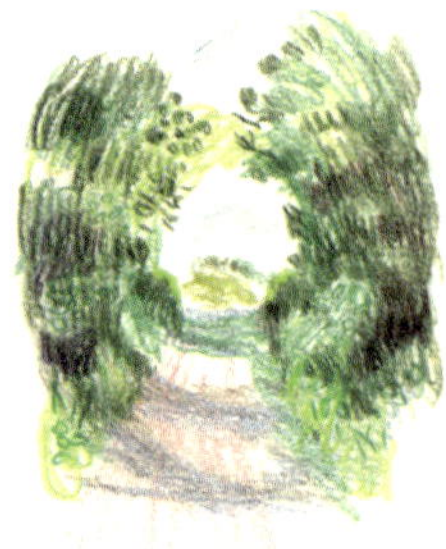

If you can look straight down a road, the lines along the rooftops on each side will converge at a vanishing point roughly in the middle of the drawing. If you look to one side, your vanishing point will also move to the side. Distances between things appear smaller the farther into the distance they are.

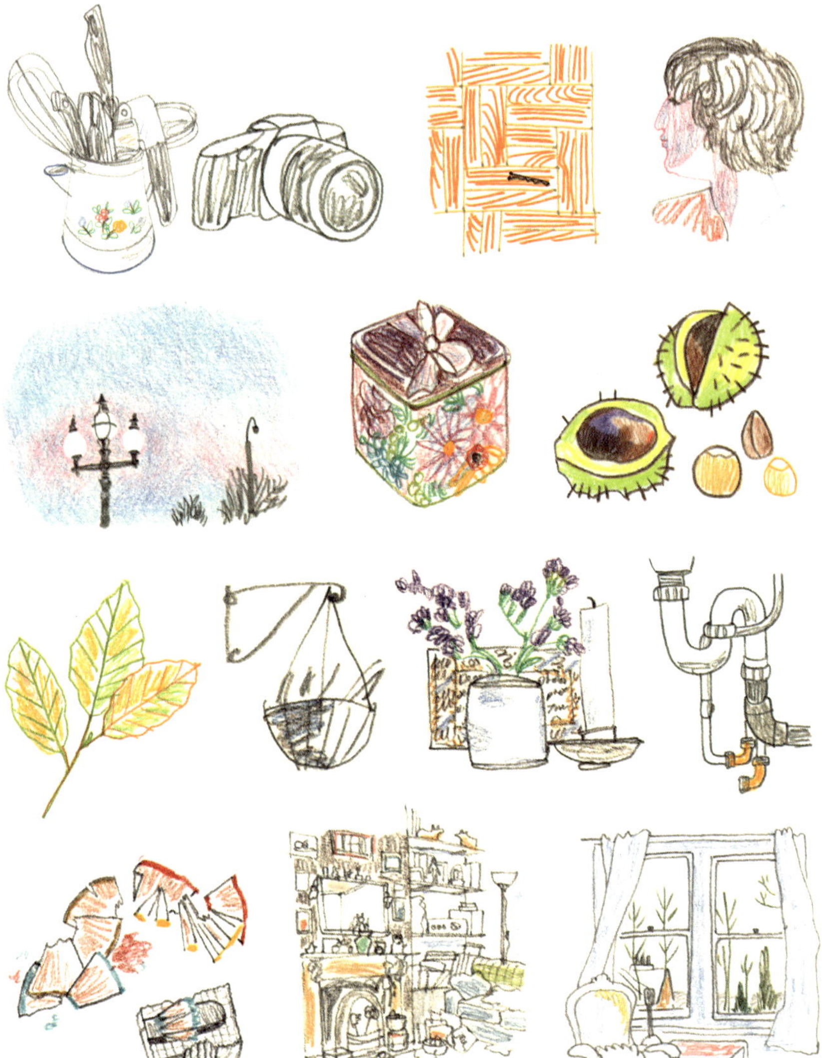

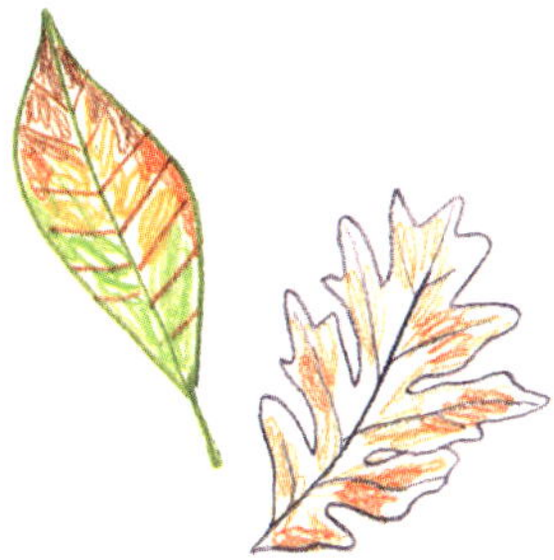

Fall

As the evenings get longer, look for streetlights going on earlier and plants and trees dropping dried-out seeds in all kinds of shapes and textures. Notice the riot of color as the leaves turn from green to oranges and browns and start to cover the ground in thick layers as they fall from the branches. As the season wears on, it's time to start thinking about what you can find to draw in the home: have a look for containers, see what you've piled up in the corners, and uncover the things you've collected in your pockets.

GADGETS, APPLIANCES & UTENSILS

Draw anything with a useful purpose, from cameras to lemon squeezers. You can choose to focus on items in the kitchen, and draw cutlery, pots, pans, and other cooking apparatus, or look around the rest of your house for other gadgets: routers, staplers, hair dryers, phones, or clocks. Do you have any old appliances gathering dust that would be interesting to draw?

You can draw objects as you find them, or arrange them more purposefully. If the objects you want to draw are complicated in shape or detail, simplify them by using just one or two colors for each drawing.

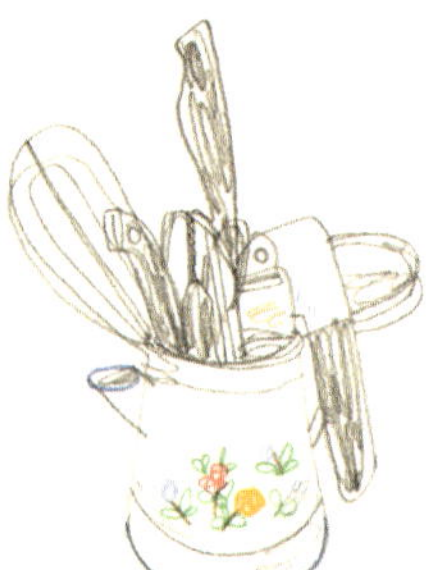

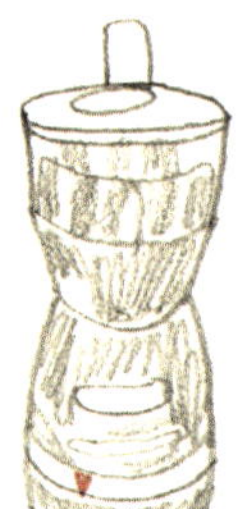

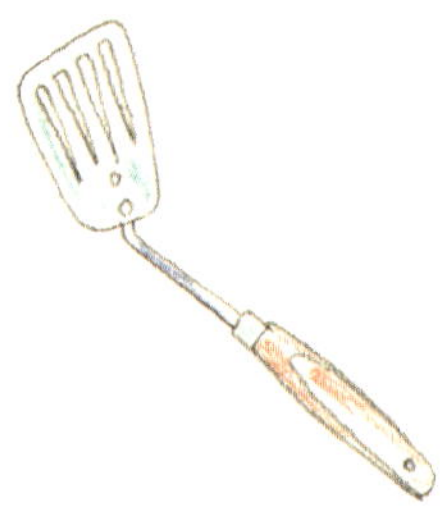

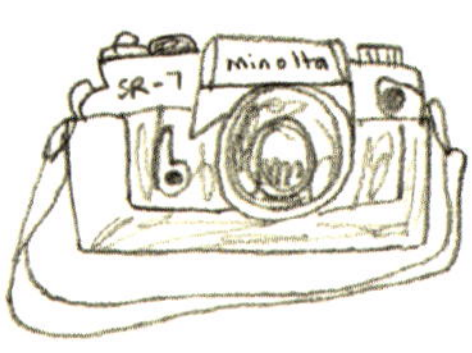

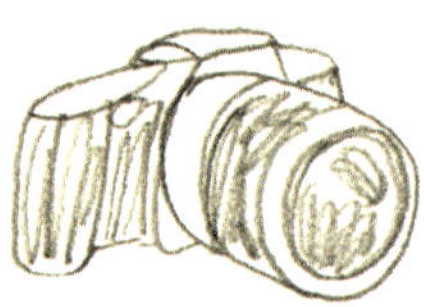

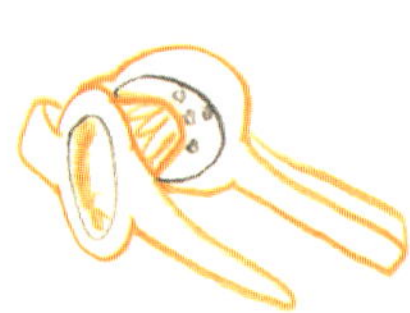

TILE PATTERNS

Look for tile patterns inside or outside buildings, or at home. They might be mosaic, lino, cork, concrete, ceramic, or marble. Are they minimal, geometric, tacky, polished, or dirty? Color loosely using markers, letting white patches show through. Don't worry about coloring right up to any outlines. This will keep colors bright and give a sense of movement.

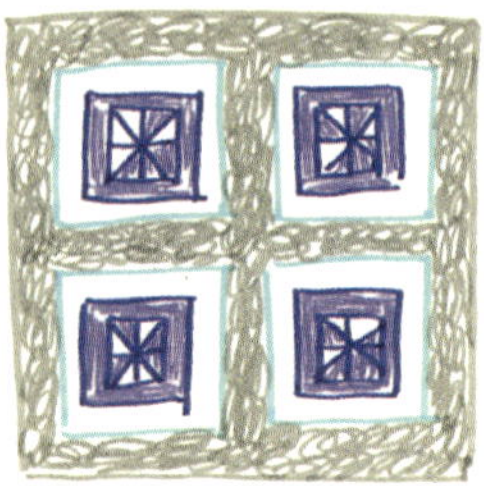

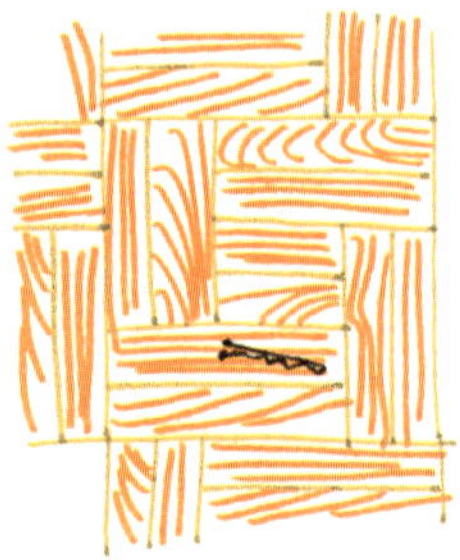

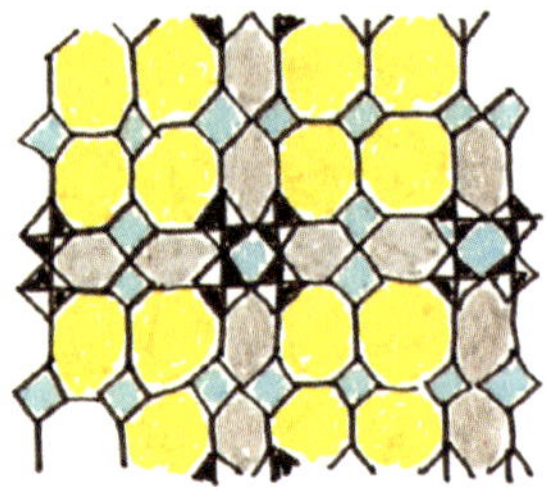

When I tried drawing the wood laminate bathroom tiles, it was cold so I drew quickly. The faucet was leaking and I couldn't help drawing the grain in time with the drips. I drew a hairpin that was on the tiles; you can add whatever is around. The more complicated pattern is from a photo. As you complete your grid, your tiles will make tiles of tiles.

PROFILES

When drawing someone in profile, before you make any marks, really look carefully at the line that the edge of their face makes. What would they look like in silhouette? Try not to see this line as part of a face but as an abstract zigzag that follows the contours of their forehead, nose, top lip, bottom lip, and chin.

You can stylize or oversimplify your drawings on purpose using limited colors; one for the profile and a different color or colors for their eyes, hair, glasses, or shadows. Look for hairstyles that make interesting shapes when seen from the side.

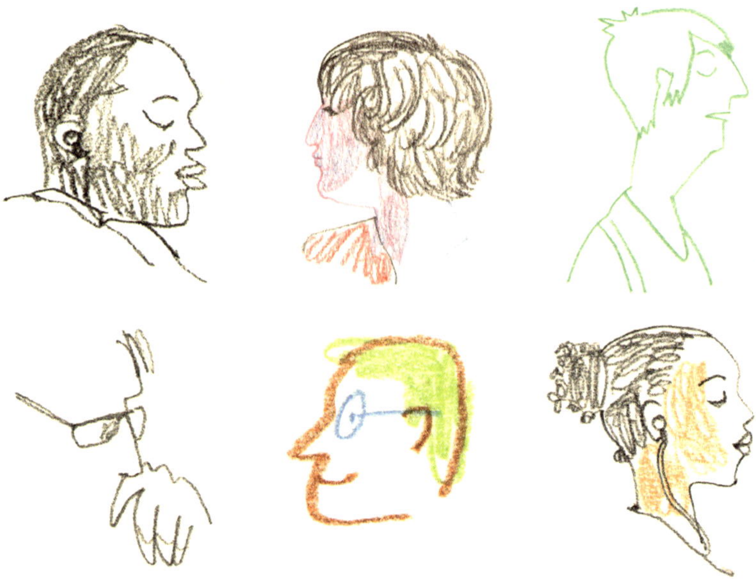

STREETLIGHTS

When streetlights first come on in the evening, there's still enough natural light for the lamppost to appear silhouetted, while the bulb also glows brightly. If you're drawing at this time, try leaving the lamp part of your sketch empty and color or shade the sky around it; without an outline, the bulb will look like it's shining.

If drawing multiple streetlights, measure them against each other to help get proportions right. Where does the shortest post come up to on the tallest? Are they all the same distance apart? Vary the thicknesses of the lines; thinner lines will appear farther away.

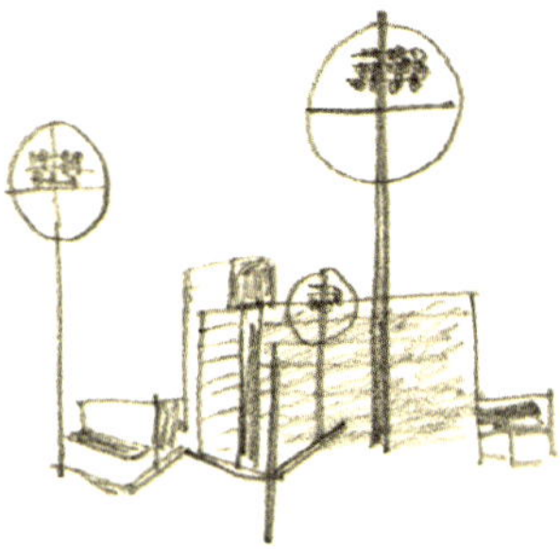

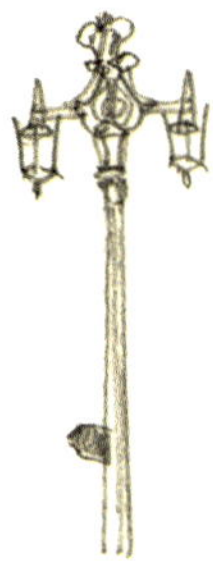

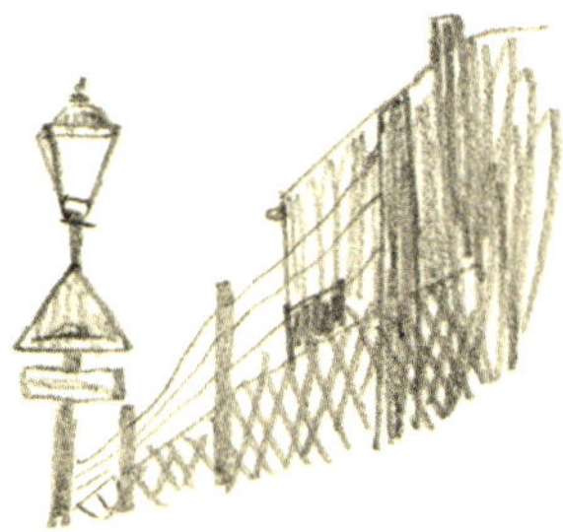

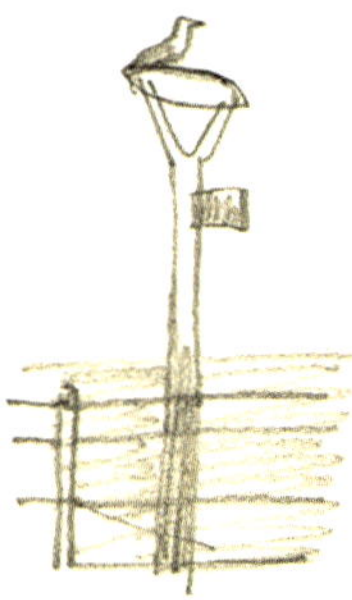

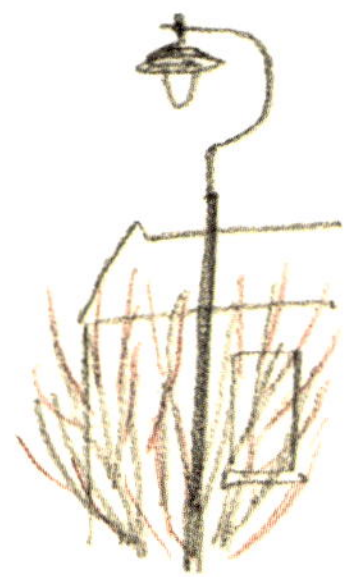

CONTAINERS

Look for jars, pots, pans, pitchers, or vases—any type of vessel. Are they full? Can you see what's inside? Are they decorative or practical? Do they have any kind of pattern? If they do have some decoration, first try drawing the basic shape of the vessel before adding it. You can arrange a couple of containers to draw at the same time; are there any that look good together? If you have to choose one color to draw the shadow, what would it be?

I really enjoyed drawing these. Oddly shaped vessels were easier to draw than those of a more regular shape, such as a saucepan—I guess because it's more noticeable if the regular shape isn't exactly right. But don't be deterred by drawing saucepans as well.

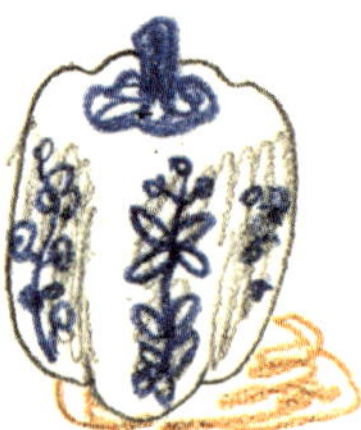

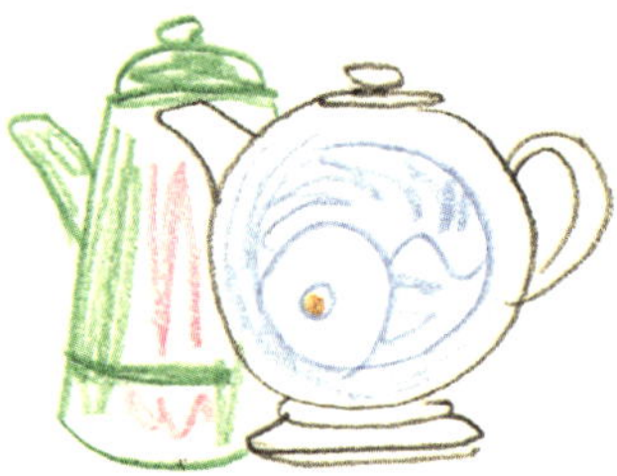

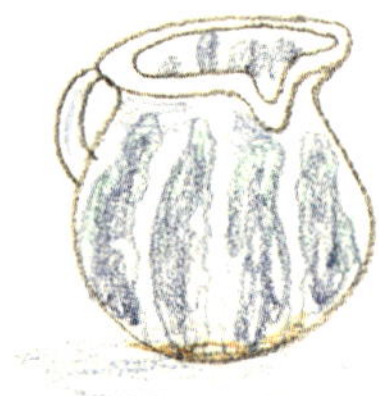

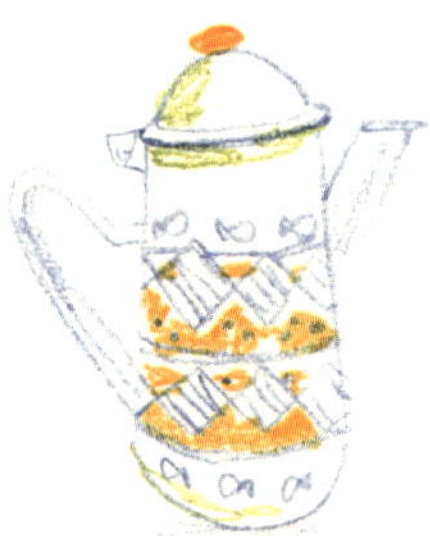

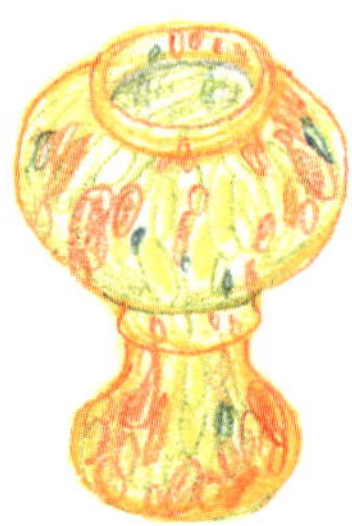

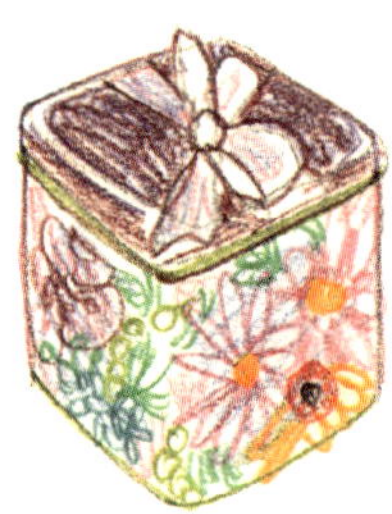

SEEDS

Look for hues in the seeds that you might not expect to be there. We know that horse chestnuts are brown, but the darkest parts can reflect an almost bluey-purple light. Look for acorns with their hats pulled down low, tiny empty cups, fluffy ball-type things or "oak gall" (when a wasp lays an egg inside an acorn and an interesting lump grows around it). Other seeds look like old men with beards. Some seed heads turn almost completely black and furry—you could do these with a scratchy pen.

With many of these, I first added a blob of color, then I quickly penciled in a more defined shape and some detail over the top. I used cool dark brown, warm mid-brown, and cool purple to draw the seed in its casing. If you press quite hard while twisting the pencil, you can make a gnarly, natural-looking line.

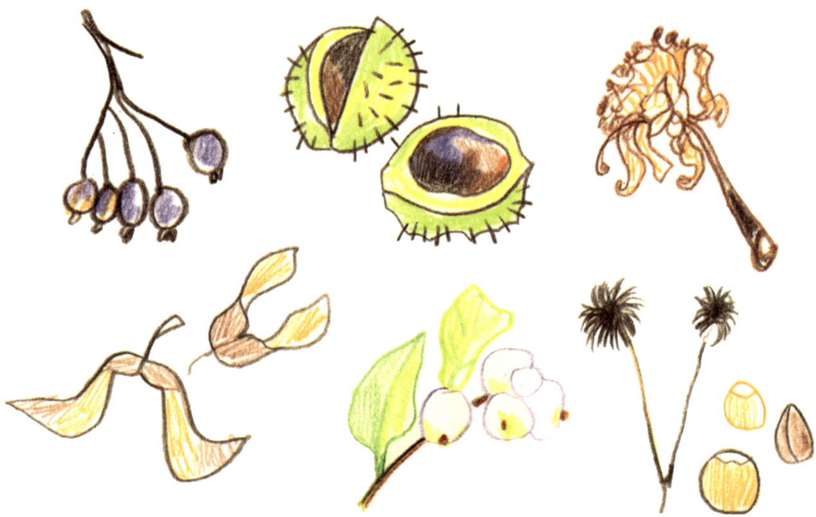

LEAVES

Pick up or photograph any colorful leaves that you find on the ground, or draw them still on the tree. Fall is obviously the best time to find colorful leaves, but this is still a good exercise for any time of year. Look for spots and patches of color, and for crumpled, folded-up, or squashed leaves, as well as perfect examples.

I first roughly sketched an outline, then I added veins and loosely added other colors. Even if a leaf looks as if it's all one color, study it closely—what color are the veins? Does the leaf have a shiny surface that reflects light, or does it curl and create areas of shadow?

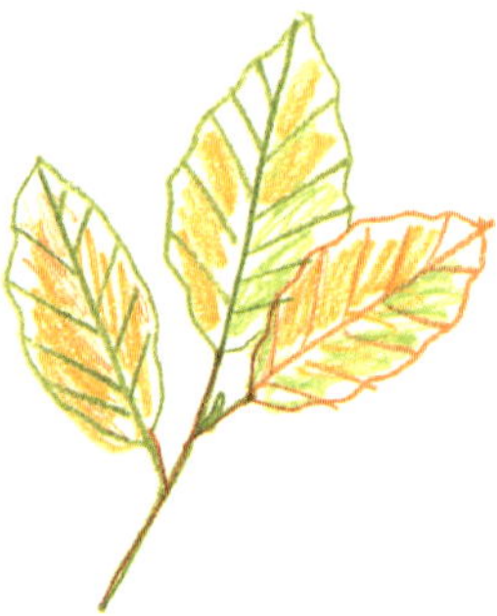
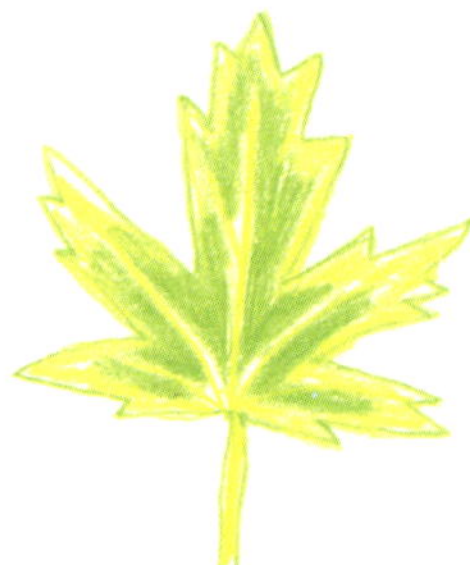

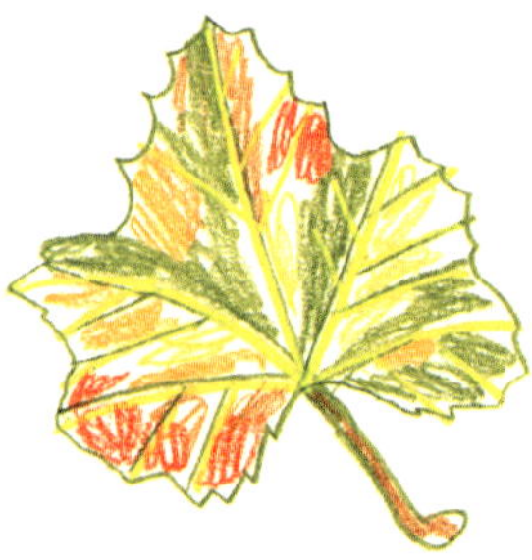
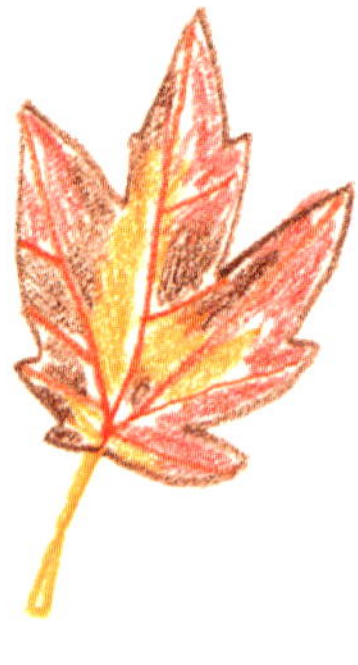
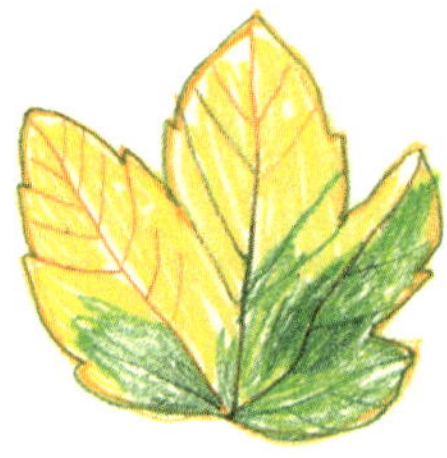

EXTERNAL FIXTURES

Have a look at the things that have been attached to the outside of domestic or commercial buildings—extractor fans, boxes for electrical cables, alarm systems, surveillance cameras, or anything else that you think looks interesting. You can choose to collect drawings of just one thing, for example satellite dishes, or look for a variety.

Think about what to omit from these drawings. You can choose to make a simple sketch focusing on only a single object; you don't need to draw in the pattern made by the bricks or other parts of the surrounding building unless you want to.

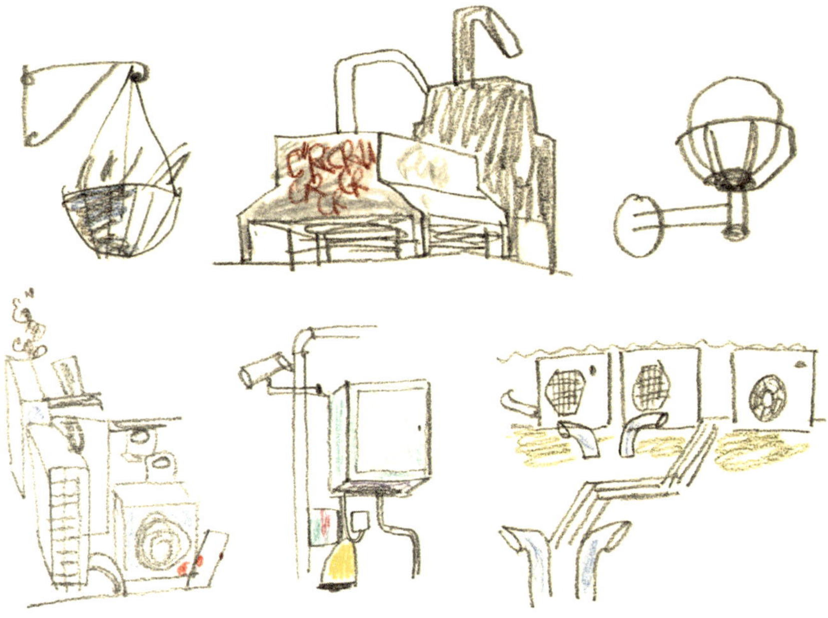

ACCIDENTAL ARRANGEMENTS

Look for things that have been put side-by-side unintentionally, or stacked on top of each other. These can be small household objects—I just drew whatever happened to be on my table and shelves—or larger collections of things outside, such as building materials or rows of recycling containers.

What kind of shape do all the things make when they are grouped together? Look at how each object relates to the others in these accidental still lifes. Which is the most prominent object? Will you make it stand out by using a different material or color?

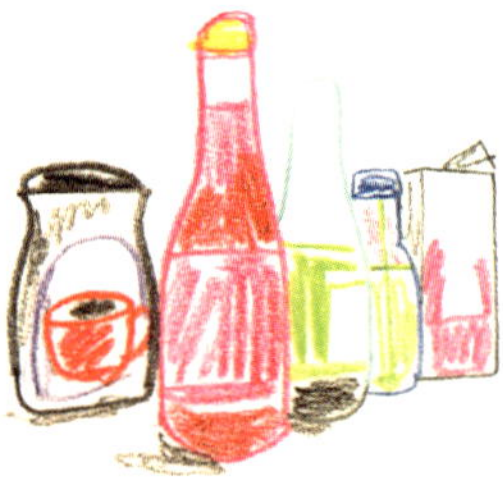

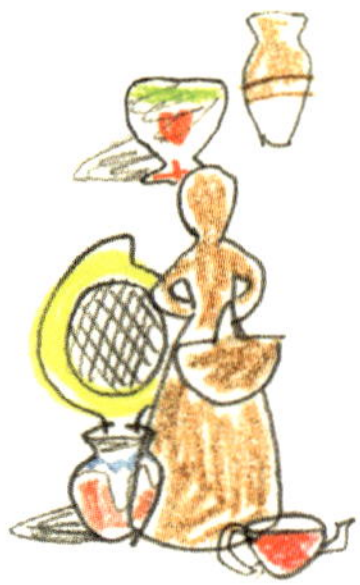

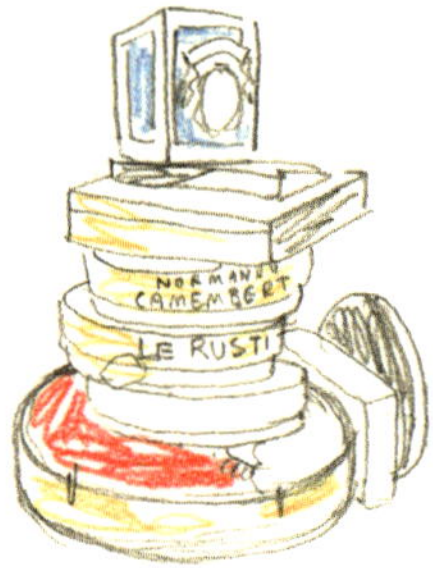

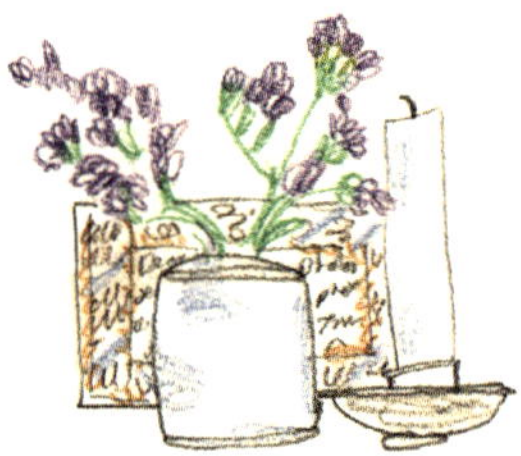

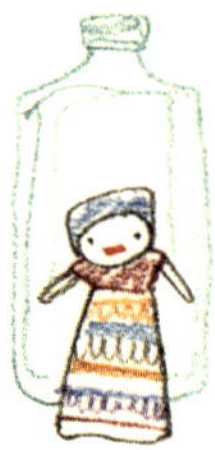

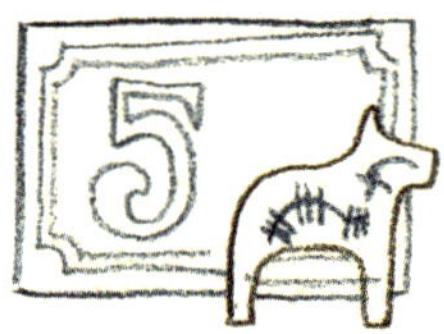

PIPE JOINTS

Under your kitchen sink, around your boiler or furnace, or stuck to the outside of your house, you'll find pipe joints. Mysterious intersections, their routes defined by the laws of gravity. Altogether, a full grid of pipe-joint drawings will start to look like a strange machine. If your house is modern and pipes are concealed, look for them in public places, restrooms, staff rooms, or on the outside of older buildings.

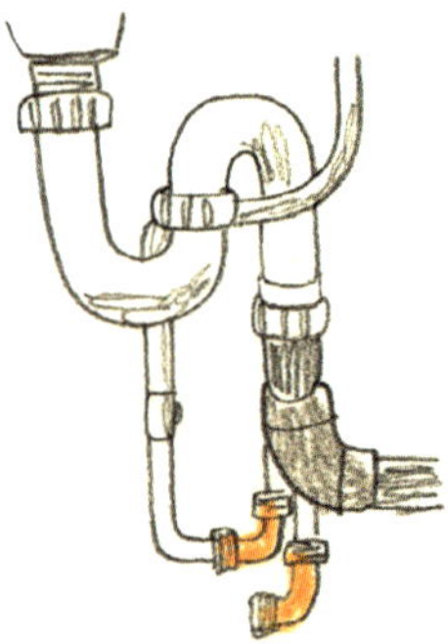

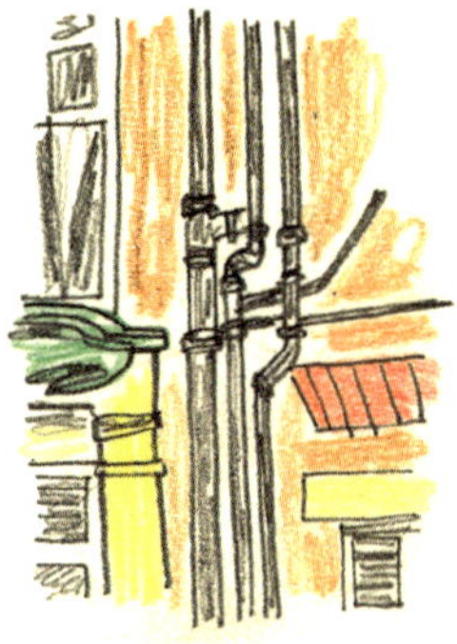

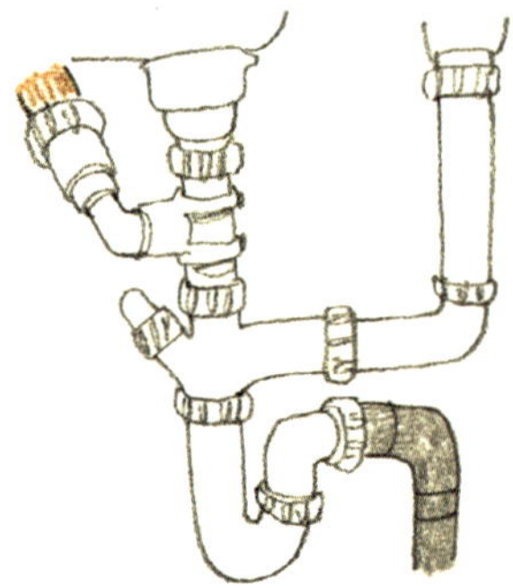

It will be interesting to crop out the rest of the building and just focus on the pipes. On their own, they look weirdly disembodied, like alien limbs or an exoskeleton. Are the pipes monochrome, or do any components have a color? You can simplify your drawings by using just one color and a graphite pencil, as I have done for the larger pipes, or stylize by using completely different colors from the ones you can see.

POCKET-SIZED OBJECTS

Draw the things that are in your pockets, such as pieces of fluff, receipts, coins, and other odds and ends. You can also draw other small things around the place that are pocket-sized even if you'd never find them in your pockets—cloves of garlic, feathers, lids, marbles, barrettes, or other detritus.

I always have a lot of this kind of stuff in my house! If you're tidier than me, you might not have so much, but you can start to collect some things to draw that you would otherwise throw away. You can use a single item for a quick sketch, or group a few together for a more colorful and detailed composition.

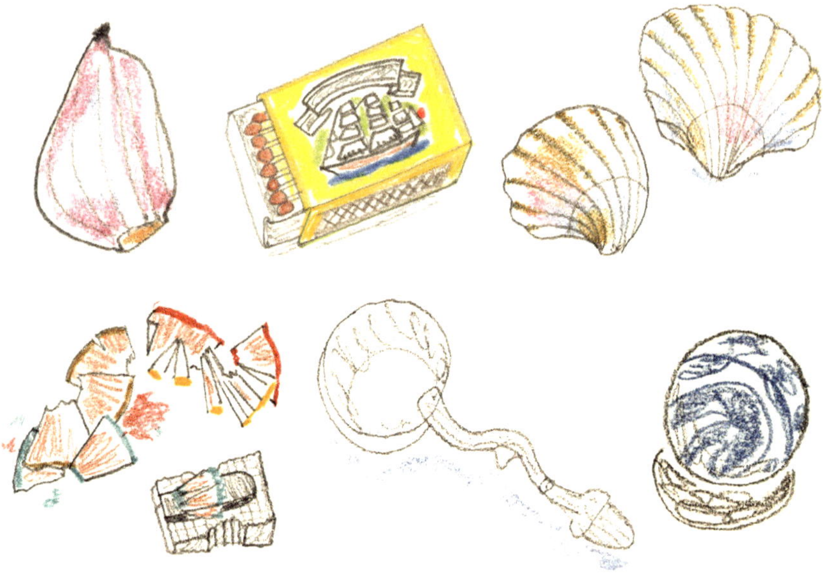

CORNERS OF ROOMS

Have a look at how furniture and objects are arranged in the corners of the rooms where you live or work. Are they tidy and ordered, or are there cascading piles of stuff? Is it a corner you don't look at often or one you're familiar with? If the area is cluttered, simplify some of the detail by including only a suggestion of what you can see.

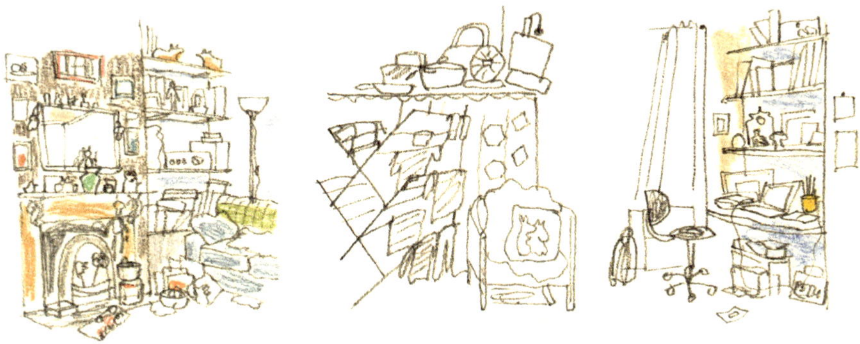

I didn't draw every book above my desk; I just added a few lines that immediately suggest "books" when you look at them. Will you draw the corners as they are, or first tidy and rearrange things? Notice light and shadows too—the area underneath shelves will be darker.

WINDOWS FROM THE INSIDE

You can use a window to frame a view of what's outside. Moving around the room, your view inside the window frame will change. Find a position that creates a composition that you want to draw. Is there anything in front of the window that you can include? Is the room darker than the view? Is there a far-reaching view, or one of an opposite window or wall? Is the view abstract, of brick patterns, texture, or glass, or does it contain objects such as trees, fences, roofs, chimneys, or horizons?

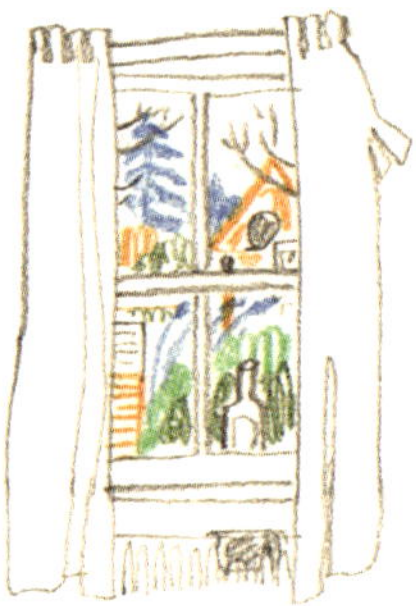
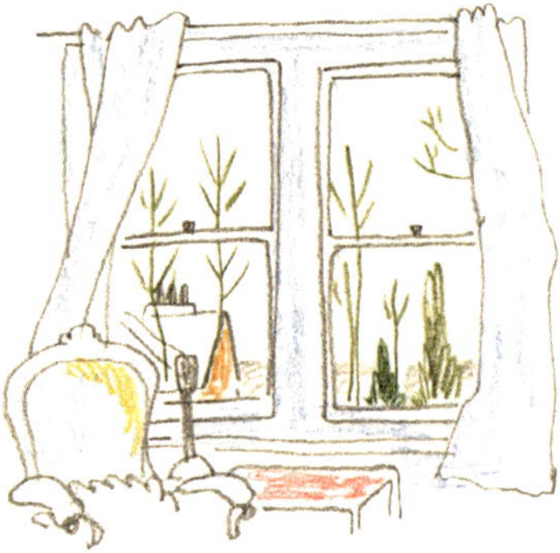
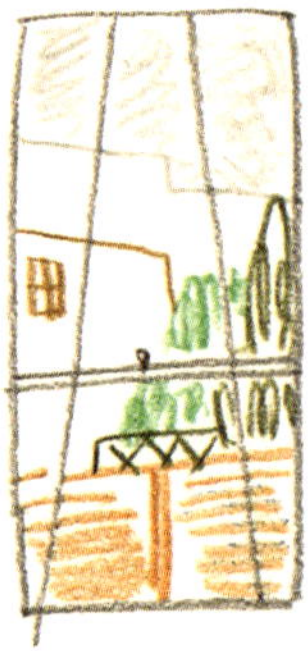

If the view contains a lot of detail, you can decide on a way to simplify your drawing. Which part of this view will you include? Will you use color or not? You can use just one color or material for inside the room and another color or material for the view.

Acknowledgments

Huge "thank you" to the following people for allowing me to draw their things, and for having long conversations with me about drawing: Victoria Trinder, Vicki Fornieles, Claire Harmer, Amy Liptrot, Mully and Helen Jowers, Tom Duxbury, Ben Austwick, Elinor Cooper, Adam Hennessey, Alan Bennett, Cesca Dvorak, Joe Mann, Lucy Fisher, Tom Fisher, Jill Gibbon, Emma Tristram, Michelle Edwards, Henri Beadle, Rebecca Davies, Pascal Anson, Cathy Gale, the Deptford is Forever project, and my students at Kingston University.

I'd also like to thank Monica Perdoni for asking me to write this book, and Tom Kitch and Michael Whitehead for helping me to make it.

And my grandmother, Felicity Fisher, for inspiring me to draw in the first place.

Matilda Tristram

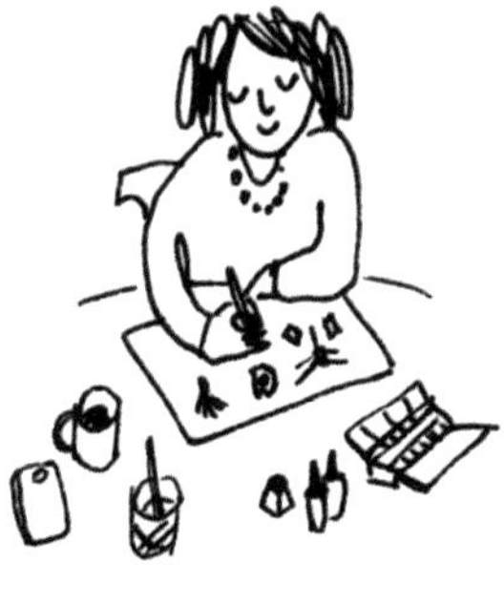